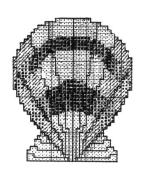

Charted
Seashell Designs

by Barbara Christopher

Dover Publications, Inc., New York

As always, to my editor and friend, M. C. Waldrep.

With my most grateful appreciation to Ruth M. Murphy, Ethel (Mrs. Jack) Rowe, Mary Berry Waldrep and Patricia Rowe Dukes for giving me so many of the wonderful seashells I used as models for this book.

Copyright © 1990 by Dover Publications, Inc.
All rights reserved under Pan American and International Copyright Conventions.

Published in Canada by General Publishing Company, Ltd., 30 Lesmill Road, Don Mills, Toronto, Ontario.
Published in the United Kingdom by Constable and Company, Ltd., 10 Orange Street, London WC2H 7EG.

Charted Seashell Designs is a new work, first published by Dover Publications, Inc., in 1990.

Manufactured in the United States of America
Dover Publications, Inc., 31 East 2nd Street, Mineola, N.Y. 11501

Library of Congress Cataloging-in-Publication Data

Christopher, Barbara.
    Charted seashell designs / by Barbara Christopher.
        p.   cm. — (Dover needlework series)
    ISBN 0-486-26286-3
    1. Embroidery—Patterns. 2. Shells in art. I. Title. II. Series.
TT773.C537   1990
746.44—dc20   89-77927
                                                            CIP

Introduction

Collecting seashells has long been a favorite pastime. These delicate beauties are truly one of nature's miracles—richly detailed, often intricate and convoluted and, above all, exquisite. Even the names—Flame Auger, Magellanic Trophon, Australian Trumpet, Pagoda Shell—evoke a feeling of mystery and romance.

Now you can make your own collection of beautiful shells, even if you can't get to the seashore. Choose from over 100 varieties, including single shells, borders, frames and corners, all in a wide range of sizes.

Most of these designs were originally created for counted cross-stitch, but they are easily translated into other needlework techniques. Keep in mind that the finished piece will not be the same size as the charted design unless you are working on fabric or canvas with the same number of threads per inch as the chart has squares per inch. With knitting and crocheting, the size will vary according to the number of stitches per inch.

COUNTED CROSS-STITCH

MATERIALS

1. **Needles.** A small blunt tapestry needle, No. 24 or No. 26.

2. **Fabric.** Evenweave linen, cotton, wool or synthetic fabrics all work well. The most popular fabrics are aida cloth, linen and hardanger cloth. Cotton aida is most commonly available in 18 threads-per-inch, 14 threads-per-inch and 11 threads-per-inch (14-count is the most popular size). Evenweave linen comes in a variety of threads-per-inch. To work cross-stitch on linen involves a slightly different technique (see page 4). Thirty thread-per-inch linen will result in a stitch about the same size as 14-count aida. Hardanger cloth has 22 threads to the inch and is available in cotton or linen. The amount of fabric needed depends on the size of the cross-stitch design. To determine yardage, divide the number of stitches in the design by the thread-count of the fabric. For example: If a design 112 squares wide by 140 squares deep is worked on a 14-count fabric, divide 112 by 14 (= 8), and 140 by 14 (= 10). The design will measure 8″ × 10″. The same design worked on 22-count fabric measures about 5″ × 6½″. When cutting the fabric, be sure to allow at least 2″ of blank fabric all around the design for finishing.

3. **Threads and Yarns.** Six-strand embroidery floss, crewel wool, Danish Flower Thread, pearl cotton or metallic threads all work well for cross-stitch. DMC Embroidery Floss has been used to color-code the patterns in this volume; a conversion chart for Royal Mouliné Six-Strand Embroidery Floss from Coats & Clark, and Anchor Embroidery Floss from Susan Bates appears on page 48. Crewel wool works well on evenweave wool fabric. Danish Flower Thread is a thicker thread with a matte finish, one strand equaling two of embroidery floss.

4. **Embroidery Hoop.** A wooden or plastic 4″, 5″ or 6″ round or oval hoop with a screw-type tension adjuster works best for cross-stitch.

5. **Scissors.** A pair of sharp embroidery scissors is essential to all embroidery.

PREPARING TO WORK

To prevent raveling, either whip stitch or machine-stitch the outer edges of the fabric.

Locate the exact center of the chart (many of the charts in this book have an arrow at the top or bottom and side; follow these arrows to their intersection to locate the chart center). Establish the center of the fabric by folding it in half first vertically, then horizontally. The center stitch of the chart falls where the creases of the fabric meet. Mark the fabric center with a basting thread.

It is best to begin cross-stitch at the top of the design. To establish the top, count the squares up from the center of the chart, and the corresponding number of holes up from the center of the fabric.

Place the fabric tautly in the embroidery hoop, for tension makes it easier to push the needle through the holes without piercing the fibers. While working continue to retighten the fabric as necessary.

When working with multiple strands (such as embroidery floss) always separate (strand) the thread before beginning to stitch. This one small step allows for better coverage of the fabric. When you need more than one thread in the needle, use separate strands and do not double the thread. (For example: If you need four strands, use four separated strands.) Thread has a nap (just as fabrics do) and can be felt to be smoother in one direction than the other. Always work with the nap (the smooth side) pointing down.

For 14-count aida and 30-count linen, work with two strands of six-strand floss. For more texture, use more thread; for a flatter look, use less thread.

EMBROIDERY

To begin, fasten the thread with a waste knot and hold a short length of thread on the underside of the work, anchoring it with the first few stitches (*Diagram 1*). When the thread end is securely in place, clip the knot.

To stitch, push the needle up through a hole in the fabric, cross the thread intersection (or square) on a left-to-right diagonal (*Diagram 2*). Half the stitch is now completed.

DIAGRAM 2

Next, cross back, right to left, forming an X (*Diagram 3*).

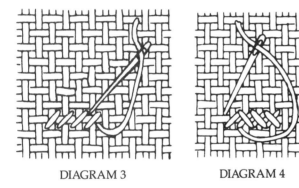

DIAGRAM 3   DIAGRAM 4

Work all the same color stitches on one row, then cross back, completing the X's (*Diagram 4*).

Some needleworkers prefer to cross each stitch as they come to it. This method also works, but be sure all of the top stitches are slanted in the same direction. Isolated stitches must be crossed as they are worked. Vertical stitches are crossed as shown in *Diagram 5*.

DIAGRAM 5

At the top, work horizontal rows of a single color, left to right. This method allows you to go from an unoccupied space to an occupied space (working from an empty hole to a filled one), making ruffling of the floss less likely. Holes are used more than once, and all stitches "hold hands" unless a space is indicated on the chart. Hold the work upright throughout (do not turn as with many needlepoint stitches).

When carrying the thread from one area to another, run the needle under a few stitches on the wrong side. Do not carry thread across an open expanse of fabric as it will be visible from the front when the project is completed.

To end a color, weave in and out of the underside of the stitches, making a scallop stitch or two for extra security (*Diagram 6*). When possible, end in the same direction in which you were working, jumping up a row if necessary (*Diagram 7*). This prevents holes caused by stitches being pulled in two directions. Trim the thread ends closely and do not leave any tails or knots as they will show through the fabric when the work is completed.

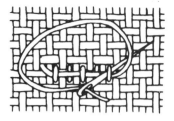

A number of other counted-thread stitches can be used in cross-stitch. Backstitch (*Diagram 8*) is used for outlines, face details and the like. It is worked from hole to hole, and may be stitched as a vertical, horizontal or diagonal line.

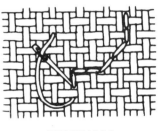

DIAGRAM 8

Straight stitch is worked from side to side over several threads (*Diagram 9*) and affords solid coverage.

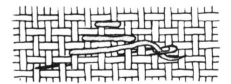

DIAGRAM 9

Embroidery on Linen. Working on linen requires a slightly different technique. While evenweave linen is remarkably regular, there are always a few thick or thin threads. To keep the stitches even, cross-stitch is worked over two threads in each direction (*Diagram 10*).

DIAGRAM 10

As you are working over more threads, linen affords a greater variation in stitches. A half-stitch can slant in either direction and is uncrossed. A three-quarters stitch is shown in *Diagram 11*.

DIAGRAM 11

Diagram 12 shows the backstitch worked on linen.

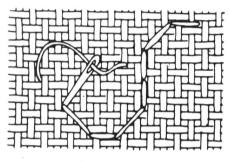

DIAGRAM 12

Embroidery on Gingham. Gingham and other checked fabrics can be used for cross-stitch. Using the fabric as a guide, work the stitches from corner to corner of each check.

Embroidery on Uneven-Weave Fabrics. If you wish to work cross-stitch on an uneven-weave fabric, baste a lightweight Penelope needlepoint canvas to the material. The design can then be stitched by working the cross-stitch over the double mesh of the canvas. When working in this manner, take care not to catch the threads of the canvas in the embroidery. After the cross-stitch is completed, remove the basting threads. With tweezers remove first the vertical threads, one strand at a time, of the needlepoint canvas, then the horizontal threads.

NEEDLEPOINT

One of the most common methods for working needlepoint is from a charted design. By simply viewing each square of a chart as a stitch on the canvas, the patterns quickly and easily translate from one technique to another.

MATERIALS

1. **Needles.** A blunt tapestry needle with a rounded tip and an elongated eye. The needle must clear the hole of the canvas without spreading the threads. For No. 10 canvas, a No. 18 needle works best.

2. **Canvas.** There are two distinct types of needlepoint canvas: single-mesh (mono canvas) and double-mesh (Penelope canvas). Single-mesh canvas, the more common of the two, is easier on the eyes as the spaces are slightly larger. Double-mesh canvas has two horizontal and two vertical threads forming each mesh. The latter is a very stable canvas on which the threads stay securely in place as the work progresses. Canvas is available in many sizes, from 5 mesh-per-inch to 18 mesh-per-inch, and even smaller. The number of mesh-per-inch will, of course, determine the dimensions of the finished needlepoint project. A 60 square × 120 square chart will measure 12″ × 24″ on 5 mesh-to-the-inch canvas, 5″ × 10″ on 12 mesh-to-the-inch canvas. The most common canvas size is 10 to the inch.

3. **Yarns.** Persian, crewel and tapestry yarns all work well on needlepoint canvas.

PREPARING TO WORK

Allow 1″ to 1½″ blank canvas all around. Bind the raw edges of the canvas with masking tape or machine-stitched double-fold bias tape.

There are few hard-and-fast rules on where to begin the design. It is best to complete the main motif, then fill the background as the last step.

For any guidelines you wish to draw on the canvas, take care that your marking medium is waterproof. Nonsoluble inks, acrylic paints thinned with water so as not to clog the mesh, and waterproof felt-tip pens all work well. If unsure, experiment on a scrap of canvas.

When working with multiple strands (such as Persian yarn) always separate (strand) the yarn before beginning to stitch. This one small step allows for better coverage of the canvas. When you need more than one piece of yarn in the needle, use separate strands and do not double the yarn. For example: If you need two strands of 3-ply Persian yarn, use two separated strands. Yarn has a nap (just as fabrics do) and can be felt to be smoother in one direction than the other. Always work with the nap (the smooth side) pointing down.

For 5 mesh-to-the-inch canvas, use six strands of 3-ply yarn; for 10 mesh-to-the-inch canvas, use three strands of 3-ply yarn.

STITCHING

Cut yarn lengths 18″ long. Begin needlepoint by holding about 1″ of loose yarn on the wrong side of the work and working the first several stitches over the loose end to secure it. To end a piece of yarn, run it under several completed stitches on the wrong side of the work.

There are hundreds of needlepoint stitch variations, but tent stitch is universally considered to be *the* needlepoint stitch. The most familiar versions of tent stitch are half-cross stitch, continental stitch and basket-weave stitch.

Half-cross stitch (*Diagram 13*) is worked from left to right. The canvas is then turned around and the return row is again stitched from left

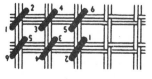

DIAGRAM 13

to right. Holding the needle vertically, bring it to the front of the canvas through the hole that will be the bottom of the first stitch. Keep the stitches loose for minimum distortion and good coverage. Half-cross stitch is best worked on a double-mesh canvas.

DIAGRAM 14

Continental stitch (*Diagram 14*) begins in the upper right-hand corner and is worked from right to left. The needle is slanted and always brought out a mesh ahead. The resulting stitch appears as a half-cross stitch on the front and as a slanting stitch on the back. When the row is complete, turn the canvas around to work the return row, continuing to stitch from right to left.

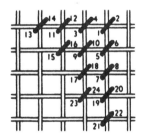

DIAGRAM 15

Basket-weave stitch (*Diagram 15*) begins in the upper right-hand corner with four continental stitches (two stitches worked horizontally across the top and two placed directly below the first stitch). Work diagonal rows, the first slanting up and across the canvas from right to left, and the next down and across from left to right. Moving down the canvas from left to right, the needle is in a vertical position; working in the opposite direction, the needle is horizontal. The rows interlock, creating a basket-weave pattern on the wrong side. If the stitch is not done properly, a faint ridge will show where the pattern was interrupted. On basket-weave stitch, always stop working in the middle of a row, rather than at the end, so that you will know in which direction you were working.

KNITTING

Charted designs can be worked into stockinette stitch as you are knitting, or they can be embroidered with duplicate stitch when the knitting is complete. For the former, wind the different colors of yarn on bobbins and work in the same manner as in Fair Isle knitting. A few quick Fair Isle tips: (1) Always bring up the new color yarn from under the dropped color to prevent holes. (2) Carry the color not in use loosely across the wrong side of the work, but not more than three or four stitches without twisting the yarns. If a color is not in use for more than seven or eight stitches, it is usually best to drop that color yarn and rejoin a new bobbin when the color is again needed.

CROCHET

There are a number of ways in which charts can be used for crochet. Among them are:

SINGLE CROCHET

Single crochet is often seen worked in multiple colors. When changing colors, always pick up the new color for the last yarn-over of the old color. The color not in use can be carried loosely across the back of the work for a few stitches, or you can work the single crochet over the unused color. The latter method makes for a neater appearance on the wrong side, but sometimes the old color peeks through the stitches. This method can also be applied to half-double crochet and double crochet, but keep in mind that the longer stitches will distort the design.

FILET CROCHET

This technique is nearly always worked from charts and uses only one color thread. The result is a solid-color piece with the design filled in and the background left as an open mesh. Care must be taken in selecting the design, as the longer stitch causes distortion.

AFGHAN CROCHET

The most common method here is cross-stitch worked over the afghan stitch. Complete the afghan crochet project. Then, following the chart for color placement, work cross-stitch over the squares of crochet.

OTHER CHARTED METHODS

Latch hook, Assisi embroidery, beading, cross-stitch on needlepoint canvas (a European favorite) and lace net embroidery are among the other needlework methods worked from charts.

Alphabetical List of Shells

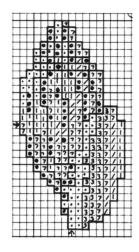

▲ MITER-SHAPED VOLUTE

15 stitches by 29 stitches

BACK-STITCH	CROSS-STITCH	DMC #	
——	◉	310	Black
	3	640	Very Dark Beige Gray
	7	642	Dark Beige Gray
	∕	644	Medium Beige Gray
	•	712	Cream
	I	822	Light Beige Gray

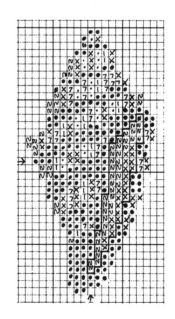

▲ RUGOSE MITER

19 stitches by 37 stitches

BACK-STITCH	CROSS-STITCH	DMC #	
——	◉	310	Black
	✕	317	Pewter Gray
	7	318	Light Steel Gray
	ℕ	413	Dark Pewter Gray
	I	415	Pearl Gray
	•		White

▼ LIGHTNING WHELK

19 stitches by 37 stitches

BACK-STITCH	CROSS-STITCH	DMC #	
——		310	Black
	⊟	402	Very Light Mahogany
	∕	945	Light Apricot
	•	951	Very Light Apricot
	ℕ	976	Medium Golden Brown
	7	977	Light Golden Brown
•◆•	◉	3031	Very Dark Mocha Brown
	3	3032	Medium Mocha Brown
	I	3033	Very Light Mocha Brown

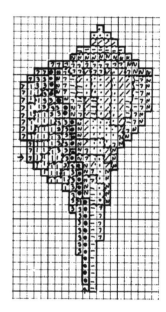

▼ LITTLE BEAR CONCH

19 stitches by 27 stitches

BACK-STITCH	CROSS-STITCH	DMC #	
——	◉	310	Black
	ℕ	318	Light Steel Gray
	I	415	Pearl Gray
	∕	725	Topaz
	◎	783	Christmas Gold
	•		White

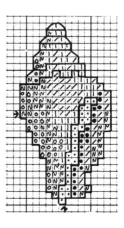

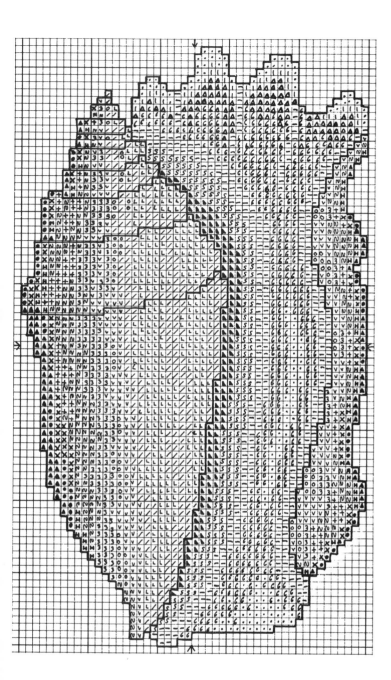

◀ LACINIATED CONCH

50 stitches by 83 stitches

BACK-STITCH	CROSS-STITCH	DMC #	
•		225	Light Shell Pink
—		310	Black
	S	315	Dark Antique Mauve
	⊟	316	Medium Antique Mauve
	H	318	Light Steel Gray
	▲	414	Dark Steel Gray
	N	415	Pearl Gray
	X	433	Medium Brown
	+	434	Light Brown
	3	435	Very Light Brown
	O	436	Tan
	L	437	Light Tan
	/	712	Cream
	V	762	Very Light Pearl Gray
	6	778	Light Antique Mauve
	●	801	Dark Coffee Brown
	◣	838	Very Dark Beige Brown
	A	945	Light Apricot
	I	951	Very Light Apricot

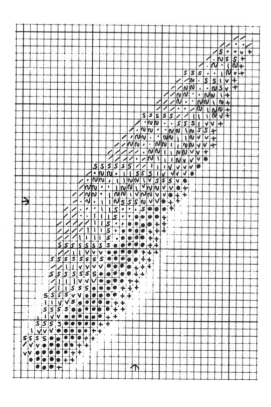

AUGER-LIKE MITER ▶

33 stitches by 47 stitches

	DMC #	
N	318	Light Steel Gray
S	407	Medium Cocoa Brown
+	632	Chocolate
•	712	Cream
I	945	Light Apricot
V	950	Light Cocoa Brown
/	951	Very Light Apricot
●	3371	Black Brown

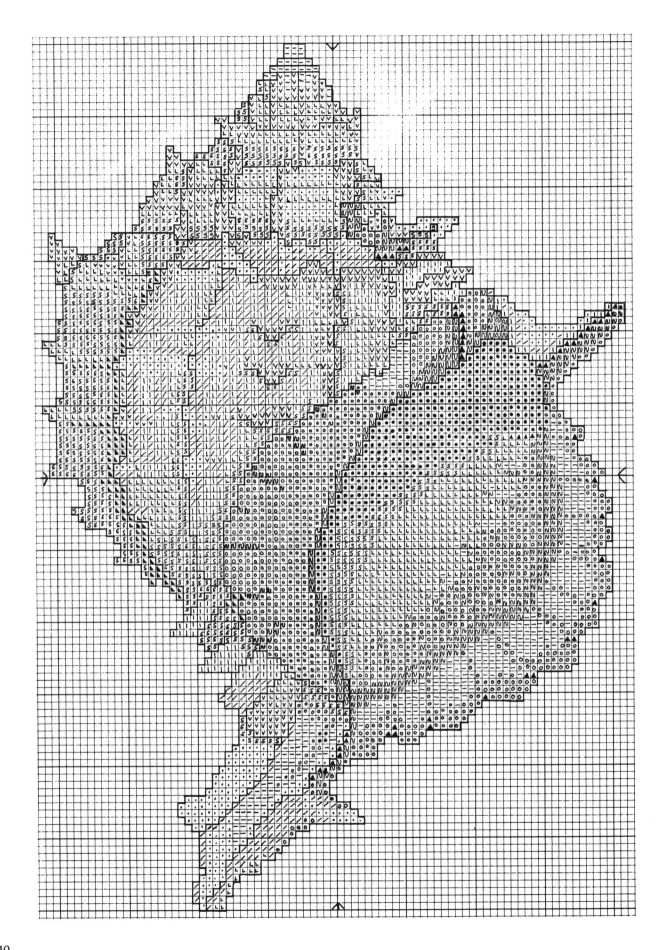

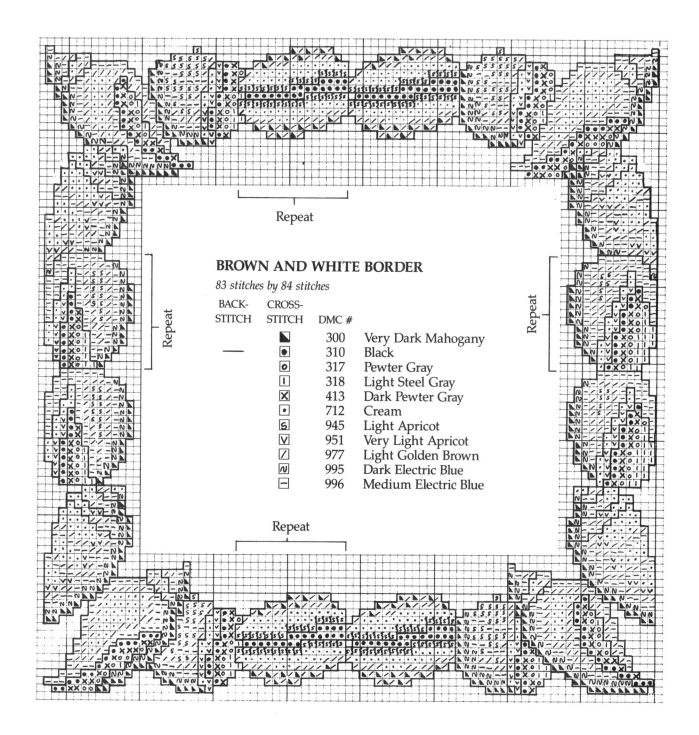

BROWN AND WHITE BORDER

83 stitches by 84 stitches

BACK-STITCH	CROSS-STITCH	DMC #	
	◣	300	Very Dark Mahogany
—	⊙	310	Black
	⊡	317	Pewter Gray
	⊞	318	Light Steel Gray
	✕	413	Dark Pewter Gray
	·	712	Cream
	⑀	945	Light Apricot
	⩔	951	Very Light Apricot
	⁄	977	Light Golden Brown
	И	995	Dark Electric Blue
	−	996	Medium Electric Blue

Repeat

Repeat

Repeat

Repeat

◀ PINK-MOUTHED MUREX

89 stitches by 120 stitches

BACK-STITCH	CROSS-STITCH	DMC #		BACK-STITCH	CROSS-STITCH	DMC #	
	⊙	221	Dark Shell Pink		◣	891	Dark Carnation Red
	⑀	223	Medium Shell Pink		⁄	950	Light Cocoa Brown
	∟	224	Light Shell Pink		·	951	Very Light Apricot
	⩔	225	Very Light Shell Pink		И	3705	Watermelon
—		310	Black		⊙	3706	Medium Watermelon
	◣	315	Dark Antique Mauve		−	3708	Light Watermelon
	⊞	407	Medium Cocoa Brown				

MIRACULOUS THATCHERIA ▶

51 stitches by 100 stitches

BACK-STITCH	CROSS-STITCH	DMC #	
——		310	Black
	o	725	Topaz
	V	726	Light Topaz
	◣	780	Very Dark Topaz
	Ͷ	782	Medium Topaz
	I	783	Christmas Gold
	●	839	Dark Beige Brown
	S	840	Medium Beige Brown
	/	841	Light Beige Brown
	·	842	Very Light Beige Brown
	−		White

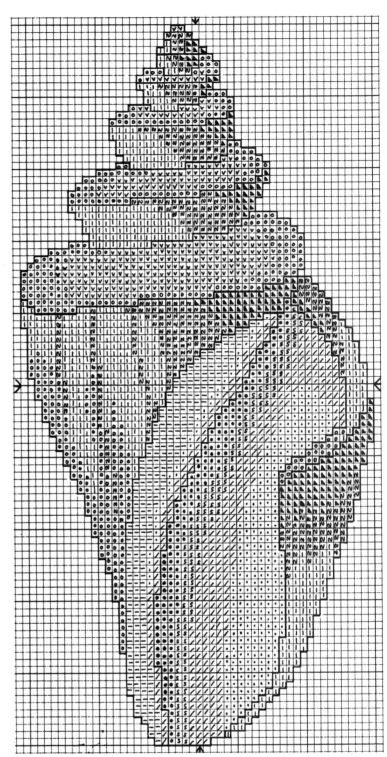

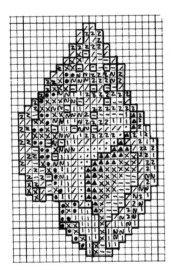

▲ FROG SHELL

21 stitches by 30 stitches

BACK-STITCH	CROSS-STITCH	DMC #	
——		310	Black
	I	407	Medium Cocoa Brown
	●	433	Medium Brown
	Ͷ	434	Light Brown
	Z	436	Tan
	/	945	Light Apricot
	·	951	Very Light Apricot
	▲	3022	Medium Brown Gray
	X	3023	Light Brown Gray
	−	3024	Very Light Brown Gray

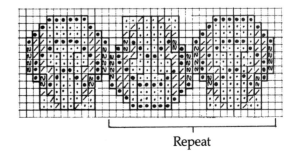

Repeat

▼ PONTIFICAL CONE

22 stitches by 30 stitches

BACK-STITCH	CROSS-STITCH	DMC #	
——		310	Black
	◉	413	Dark Pewter Gray
	Z	414	Dark Steel Gray
	I	437	Light Tan
	◣	469	Avocado Green
	N	470	Medium Light Avocado Green
	S	471	Light Avocado Green
	—	472	Very Light Avocado Green
	V	676	Light Old Gold
	▲	680	Dark Old Gold
	X	729	Medium Old Gold
	╱	738	Very Light Tan
	·	739	Fawn Beige

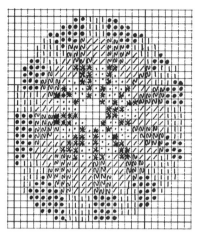

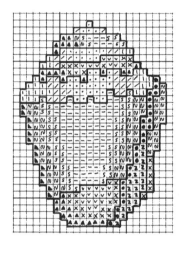

▲ PAINTED KEYHOLE LIMPET

26 stitches by 30 stitches

	DMC #	
N	433	Medium Brown
✳	434	Light Brown
I	436	Tan
╱	437	Light Tan
·	738	Very Light Tan
◉	898	Very Dark Coffee Brown

OYSTER DRILL ▶

26 stitches by 45 stitches

BACK-STITCH	CROSS-STITCH	DMC #	
——		310	Black
	S	318	Light Steel Gray
	N	413	Dark Pewter Gray
	+	414	Dark Steel Gray
	╱	738	Very Light Tan
	·	739	Fawn Beige
	◉	839	Dark Beige Brown
	X	840	Medium Beige Brown
	—	841	Light Beige Brown

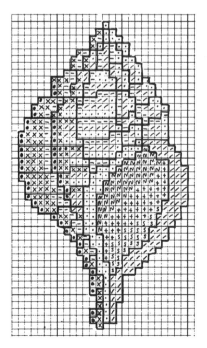

◀ ATLANTIC BAY SCALLOP

29-stitch repeat by 13 stitches

◉	610	Very Dark Drab Brown
N	3045	Dark Yellow Beige
╱	3046	Medium Yellow Beige
·	3047	Light Yellow Beige

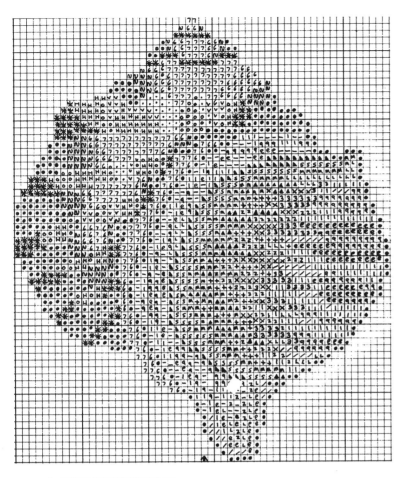

▲ GREEN TURBAN

57 stitches by 65 stitches

	DMC #	
Ⓢ	221*	Dark Shell Pink
Ⓜ	223*	Medium Shell Pink
Ⓛ	224*	Light Shell Pink
◣	300*	Very Dark Mahogany
▲	320*	Medium Pistachio Green
☒	368*	Light Pistachio Green
℮	369*	Pale Pistachio Green
◺	415*	Pearl Gray
✳	433	Medium Brown
Ⓗ	435	Very Light Brown
Ⓞ	437	Light Tan
Ⓝ	469	Avocado Green
⑥	470	Medium Light Avocado Green
⑦	471	Light Avocado Green
⊞	518*	Light Wedgwood Blue
③	519*	Sky Blue
•	712	Cream
Ⓥ	739	Fawn Beige
Ⓘ	747*	Very Light Sky Blue
⊟	776*	Medium Pink
⑨	819*	Light Baby Pink
Ⓩ	899*	Medium Rose
◉	937	Medium Avocado Green

*For an iridescent effect, combine 1 strand of Balger #032 Pearl Blending Filament with each of these colors.

▼ LIGHTNING VOLUTE

29 stitches by 60 stitches

BACK-STITCH	CROSS-STITCH	DMC #	
——		310	Black
	Ⓢ	317	Pewter Gray
	Ⓗ	318	Light Steel Gray
	⊟	402	Very Light Mahogany
	▲	413	Dark Pewter Gray
	Ⓥ	415	Pearl Gray
	●	838	Very Dark Beige Brown
	Ⓝ	839	Dark Beige Brown
	⊞	840	Medium Beige Brown
	③	841	Light Beige Brown
	Ⓛ	842	Very Light Beige Brown
	Ⓘ	945	Light Apricot
	◺	951	Very Light Apricot
	•		Ecru

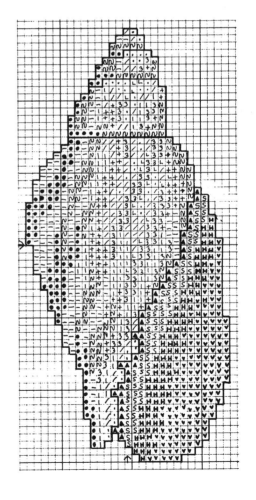

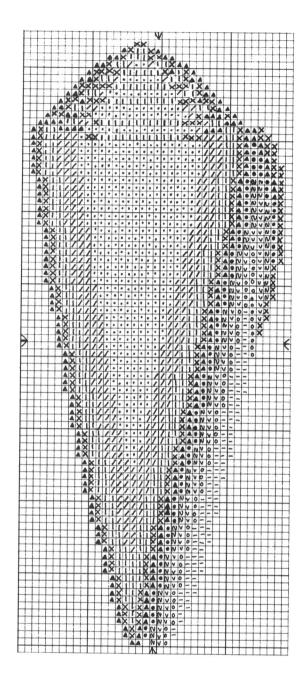

▲ VIRGIN CONE

37 stitches by 84 stitches

	DMC #	
Ⴈ	317	Pewter Gray
◎	318	Light Steel Gray
●	413	Dark Pewter Gray
Ⅴ	414	Dark Steel Gray
⊟	415	Pearl Gray
☒	760	Salmon
Ⅱ	761	Light Salmon
∕	945	Light Apricot
·	951	Very Light Apricot
▲	3328	Medium Salmon

▼ DISTAFF SPINDLE

31 stitches by 82 stitches

BACK-STITCH	CROSS-STITCH	DMC #	
——		310	Black
	Ⴈ	317	Pewter Gray
	Ⅱ	318	Light Steel Gray
	●	413	Dark Pewter Gray
	☒	414	Dark Steel Gray
	⊟	415	Pearl Gray
	∕	762	Very Light Pearl Gray
	·		White

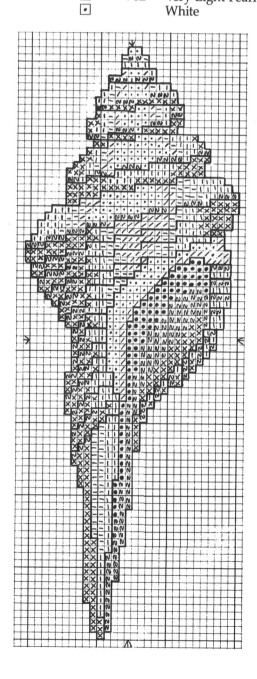

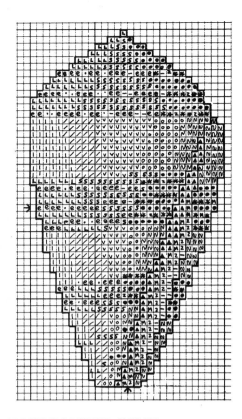

▲ ORANGE-BANDED CONE

30 stitches by 53 stitches

BACK-STITCH	CROSS-STITCH	DMC #	
	●	300	Very Dark Mahogany
———		310	Black
	M	317	Pewter Gray
	Z	318	Light Steel Gray
	▲	413	Dark Pewter Gray
	−	415	Pearl Gray
	e	433	Medium Brown
	N	720	Dark Bittersweet
	o	721	Bittersweet
	V	722	Medium Bittersweet
	✳	898	Very Dark Coffee Brown
	S	919	Red Copper
	L	921	Copper
	/	945	Light Apricot
	I	951	Very Light Apricot
	·		White

▼ AMERICAN CROWN CONCH

36 stitches by 52 stitches

BACK-STITCH	CROSS-STITCH	DMC #	
———		310	Black
	X	433	Medium Brown
	N	434	Light Brown
	V	543	Ultra Very Light Beige Brown
	·	712	Cream
	●	801	Dark Coffee Brown
	◣	840	Medium Beige Brown
	L	841	Light Beige Brown
	Z	842	Very Light Beige Brown
	I	945	Light Apricot
	/	950	Light Cocoa Brown
	−	951	Very Light Apricot
	7	3033	Very Light Mocha Brown
	o		Ecru

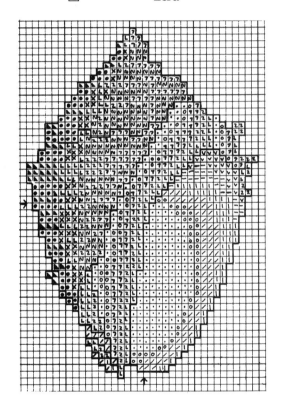

◄ PEA STRIGILLA

14-stitch repeat by 13 stitches

BACK-STITCH	CROSS-STITCH	DMC #	
	/	223	Medium Shell Pink
	−	224	Light Shell Pink
———		310	Black
	X	318	Light Steel Gray
	◣	414	Dark Steel Gray
	o	415	Pearl Gray
	●	962	Medium Dusty Rose
	N	963	Very Light Dusty Rose
	·		White

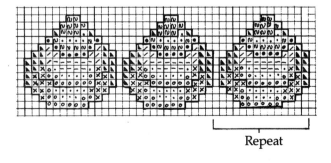

Repeat

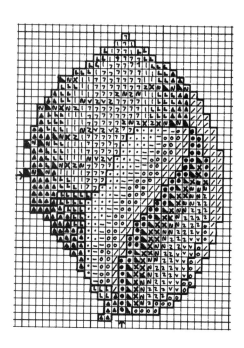

◄ PRICKLY HELMET

29 stitches by 40 stitches

BACK-STITCH	CROSS-STITCH	DMC #	
	▨	402	Very Light Mahogany
	☒	433	Medium Brown
	ℕ	434	Light Brown
	☑	435	Very Light Brown
	☑	437	Light Tan
	·	712	Cream
	◣	898	Very Dark Coffee Brown
—	●	938	Ultra Dark Coffee Brown
	◯	945	Light Apricot
	☑	950	Light Cocoa Brown
	⊟	951	Very Light Apricot
	▲	975	Dark Golden Brown
	⊡	976	Medium Golden Brown
	⊞	977	Light Golden Brown

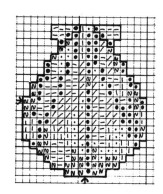

FOLDED SCALLOP ▶

18 stitches by 21 stitches

BACK-STITCH	CROSS-STITCH	DMC #	
—		310	Black
	●	318	Light Steel Gray
	☑	760	Salmon
	⊟	761	Light Salmon
	⊞	762	Very Light Pearl Gray
	ℕ	3328	Medium Salmon
	·		White

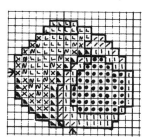

▲ GYRATE FROGSHELL

15 stitches by 23 stitches

BACK-STITCH	CROSS-STITCH	DMC #	
—		310	Black
	⊡	434	Light Brown
	⊟	543	Ultra Very Light Beige Brown
	·	712	Cream
	☒	801	Dark Coffee Brown
	⊞	841	Light Beige Brown
	☑	842	Very Light Beige Brown
	☑	3033	Very Light Mocha Brown
	●	3371	Black Brown

ROUND PERIWINKLE ▲

17 stitches by 15 stitches

BACK-STITCH	CROSS-STITCH	DMC #	
—		310	Black
	☒	469	Avocado Green
	ℕ	470	Medium Light Avocado Green
	⊡	471	Light Avocado Green
	⊞	472	Very Light Avocado Green
	☑	772	Very Light Loden Green
	●	934	Black Avocado Green
	◣	937	Burnt Orange

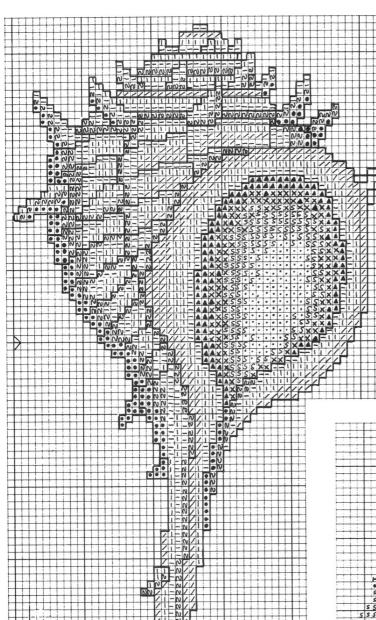

46 stitches by 74 stitches

	DMC #	
●	300	Very Dark Mahogany
S	301	Medium Mahogany
H	400	Dark Mahogany
X	402	Very Light Mahogany
I	712	Cream
O	738	Very Light Tan
–	739	Fawn Beige
◣	838	Very Dark Beige Brown
N	839	Dark Beige Brown
X	840	Medium Beige Brown
L	841	Light Beige Brown
∕	842	Very Light Beige Brown
V	945	Light Apricot
·	3033	Very Light Mocha Brown

▲ **DYE MUREX**

55 stitches by 88 stitches

BACK-STITCH	CROSS-STITCH	DMC #	
	X	327	Dark Antique Violet
	●	347	Dark Salmon
	▲	550	Dark Violet
	–	760	Salmon
	I	761	Light Salmon
	∕	945	Light Apricot
	S	3041	Medium Antique Violet
	·	3042	Light Antique Violet
	N	3328	Medium Salmon
——		3685	Dark Mauve

18

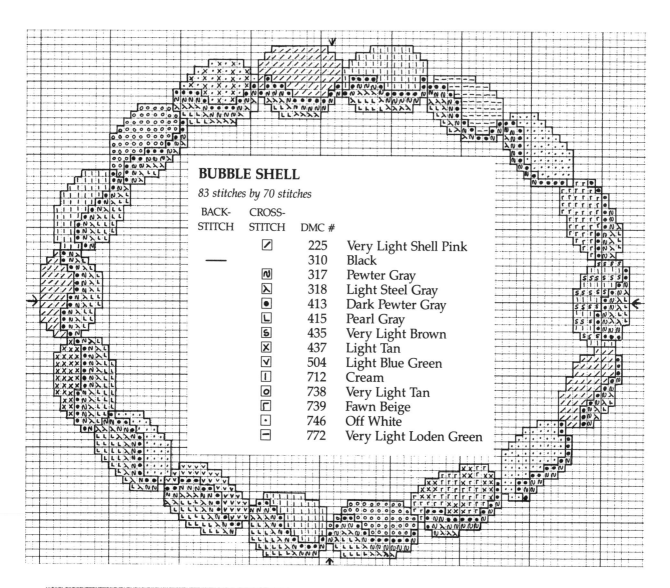

BUBBLE SHELL

83 stitches by 70 stitches

BACK-STITCH	CROSS-STITCH	DMC #	
	☑	225	Very Light Shell Pink
—		310	Black
	Ⅳ	317	Pewter Gray
	λ	318	Light Steel Gray
	⊙	413	Dark Pewter Gray
	L	415	Pearl Gray
	S	435	Very Light Brown
	X	437	Light Tan
	V	504	Light Blue Green
	I	712	Cream
	O	738	Very Light Tan
	Γ	739	Fawn Beige
	·	746	Off White
	−	772	Very Light Loden Green

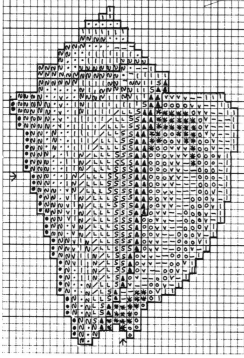

◀ FLORIDA FIGHTING CONCH

33 stitches by 47 stitches

BACK-STITCH	CROSS-STITCH	DMC #	
—		310	Black
	☑	402*	Very Light Mahogany
	⊙	646	Dark Beaver Gray
	Ⅳ	647	Medium Beaver Gray
	·	648	Light Beaver Gray
	O	721	Bittersweet
	V	722	Medium Bittersweet
	−	945	Light Apricot
	I	951	Very Light Apricot
	▲	975*	Dark Golden Brown
	S	976*	Medium Golden Brown
	L	977*	Light Golden Brown
	✳	3041	Medium Antique Violet

For an iridescent effect, combine 1 strand of Balger #021 Copper HL Blending Filament with each of these colors.

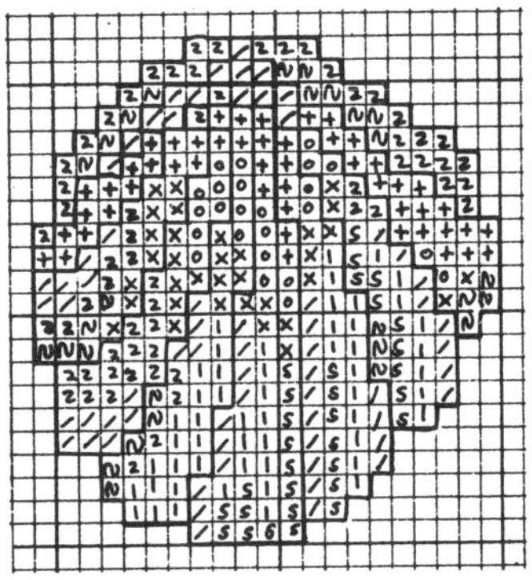

▲ PEARLY BROOCH SHELL

21 stitches by 22 stitches

BACK-STITCH	CROSS-STITCH	DMC #	
	+	208	Very Dark Lavender
	o	209	Dark Lavender
	X	210	Medium Lavender
—		310	Black
	S	518	Light Wedgwood Blue
	I	519	Sky Blue
	~	926	Dark Blue Gray
	Z	927	Medium Gray Blue
	/	928	Light Gray Blue

For an iridescent effect, combine 1 strand of Balger #032 Pearl Blending Filament with all colors except black.

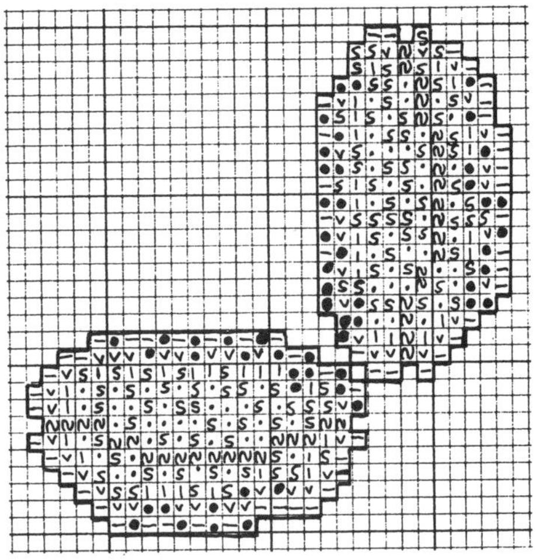

▲ PANTHER COWRIE

30 stitches by 30 stitches

BACK-STITCH	CROSS-STITCH	DMC #	
	•	300	Very Dark Mahogany
	S	301	Medium Mahogany
—		310	Black
	/	402	Very Light Mahogany
	~	420	Dark Hazelnut Brown
	−	436	Tan
	V	437	Light Tan
	I	712	Cream
	·	739	Fawn Beige

▼ ORNATE VERTICORD

28 stitches by 26 stitches

	DMC #	
•	317	Pewter Gray
~	318	Light Steel Gray
/	415	Pearl Gray
·		White

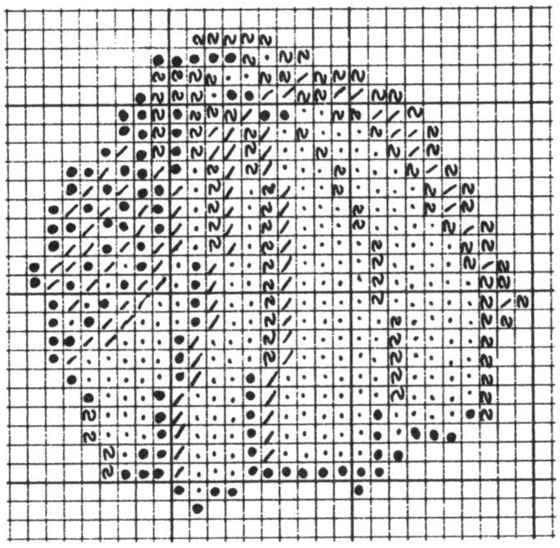

▼ TINTED CANTHARUS

15 stitches by 26 stitches

BACK-STITCH	CROSS-STITCH	DMC #	
—		310	Black
	◣	413	Dark Pewter Gray
	X	433	Medium Brown
	~	435	Very Light Brown
	−	437	Light Tan
	I	740	Tangerine
	o	741	Medium Tangerine
	/	762	Very Light Pearl Gray
	•	801	Dark Coffee Brown
	·		White

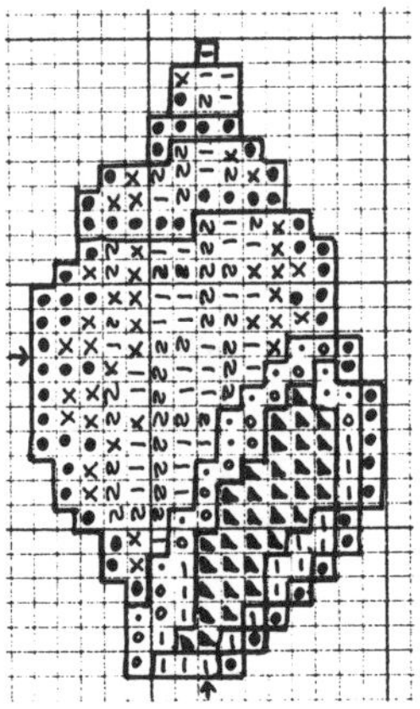

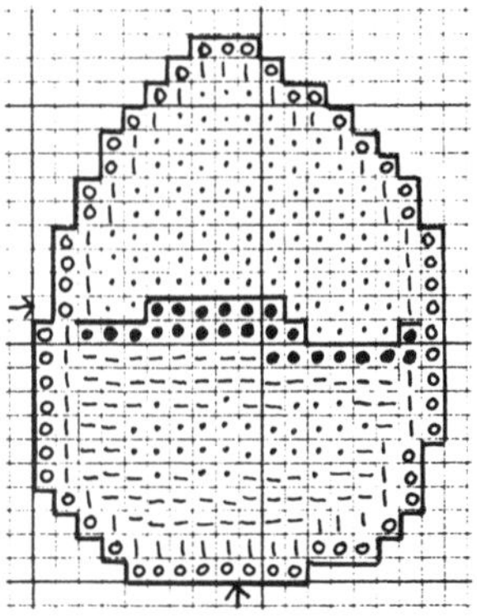

▲ EASTERN WHITE SLIPPER

18 stitches by 23 stitches

BACK-STITCH	CROSS-STITCH	DMC #	
——		310	Black
	−	371*	Pecan
	/	372*	Light Pecan
	●	420*	Dark Hazelnut Brown
	·	712	Cream
	I	739	Fawn Beige
	o		Ecru

*For an iridescent effect, combine 1 strand of Balger #100 White Blending Filament with these colors.

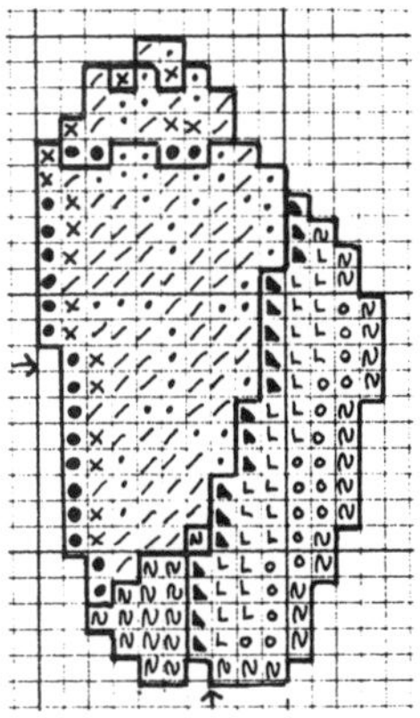

▲ BAT VOLUTE

14 stitches by 25 stitches

BACK-STITCH	CROSS-STITCH	DMC #	
——		310	Black
	N	402	Very Light Mahogany
	●	434	Light Brown
	X	436	Tan
	/	437	Light Tan
	◣	610	Very Dark Drab Brown
	L	611	Dark Drab Brown
	o	612	Medium Drab Brown
	·	738	Very Light Tan

▼ GREAT PHEASANT SHELL

14 stitches by 28 stitches

BACK-STITCH	CROSS-STITCH	DMC #	
——		310	Black
	I	318	Light Steel Gray
	✱	413	Dark Pewter Gray
	V	414	Dark Steel Gray
	●	433	Medium Brown
	Z	434	Light Brown
	N	435	Very Light Brown
	X	436	Tan
	/	437	Light Tan
	·	712	Cream
	o	738	Very Light Tan

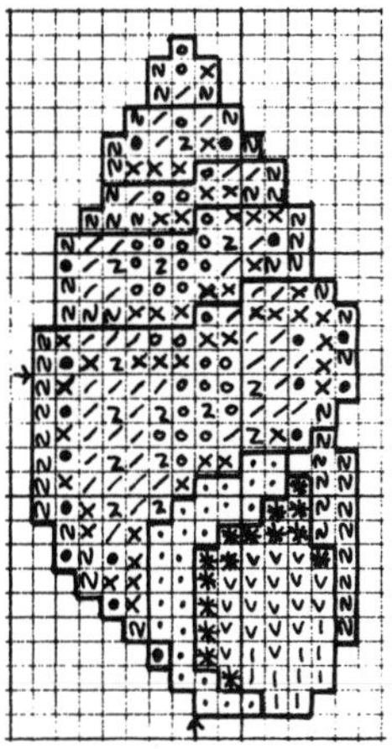

▼ THREE-LINED BASKET-SNAIL

11 stitches by 24 stitches

BACK-STITCH	CROSS-STITCH	DMC #	
——		310	Black
	●	317	Pewter Gray
	L	318	Light Steel Gray
	/	415	Pearl Gray
	o	762	Very Light Pearl Gray
	·		White

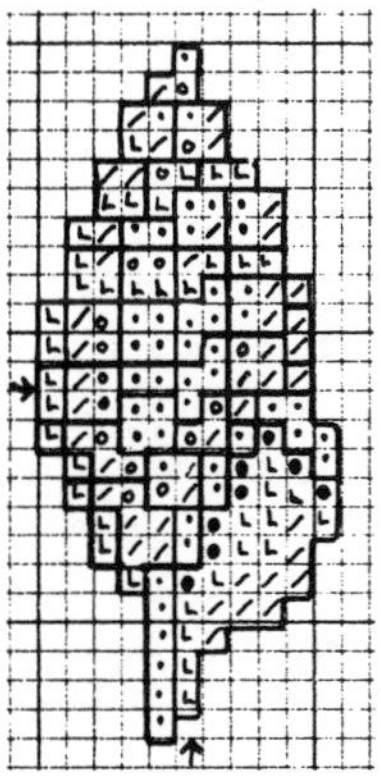

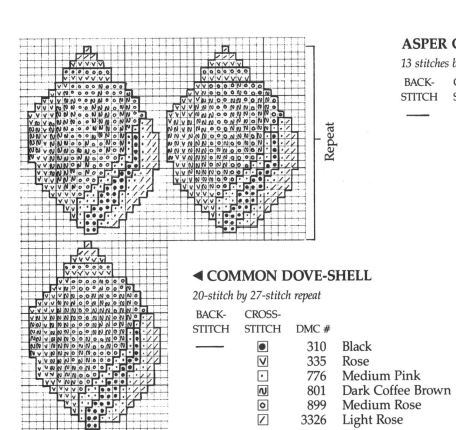

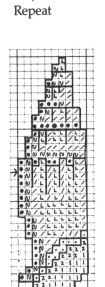

ASPER CERITH ▼

13 stitches by 26 stitches

BACK-STITCH	CROSS-STITCH	DMC #	
———		310	Black
	●	433	Medium Brown
	✕	435	Very Light Brown
	S	436	Tan
	L	437	Light Tan
	○	712	Cream
	╱	738	Very Light Tan
	·	739	Fawn Beige
	◣	3051	Dark Gray Green
	N	3052	Medium Gray Green
	I	3053	Gray Green

◀ COMMON DOVE-SHELL

20-stitch by 27-stitch repeat

BACK-STITCH	CROSS-STITCH	DMC #	
———	●	310	Black
	V	335	Rose
	·	776	Medium Pink
	N	801	Dark Coffee Brown
	○	899	Medium Rose
	╱	3326	Light Rose

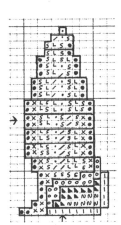

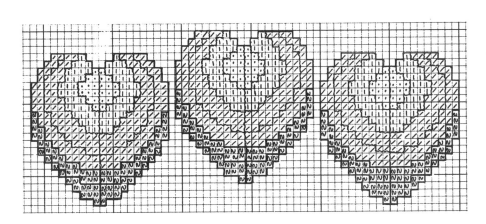

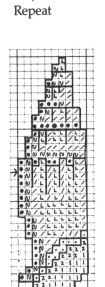

▲ COMMON VERTEGUS

10 stitches by 32 stitches

BACK-STITCH	CROSS-STITCH	DMC #	
———		310	Black
	Z	611	Dark Drab Brown
	I	612	Medium Drab Brown
	╱	676	Light Old Gold
	L	677	Very Light Old Gold
	●	680	Dark Old Gold
	·	712	Cream
	N	729	Medium Old Gold

▲ HEART COCKLE

62 stitches by 24 stitches

BACK-STITCH	CROSS-STITCH	DMC #	
	╱	725	Topaz
	I	726	Light Topaz
	·	727	Very Light Topaz
———		780	Very Dark Topaz
〜〜	N	783	Christmas Gold

◀ AUSTRALIAN TRUMPET

59 stitches by 120 stitches

BACK-STITCH	CROSS-STITCH	DMC #	
	●	300	Very Dark Mahogany
——		310	Black
	Ͷ	720	Dark Bittersweet
	3	721	Bittersweet
	−	722	Medium Bittersweet
	╱	754	Light Peach
	L	760	Salmon
	╲	761	Light Salmon
	X	919	Red Copper
	O	920	Medium Copper
	I	921	Copper
	·	948	Very Light Peach

▲ TESSELLATED NERITE

32 stitches by 12 stitches

BACK-STITCH	CROSS-STITCH	DMC #	
——	●	315	Dark Antique Mauve
	Ͷ	646	Dark Beaver Gray
	╱	647	Medium Beaver Gray
	·		White

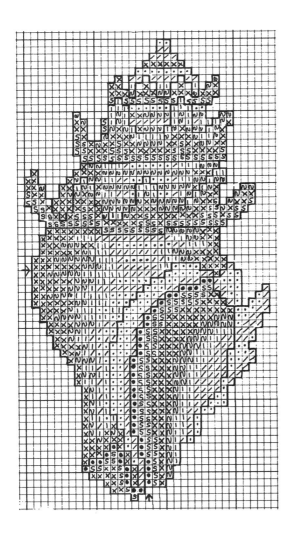

35 stitches by 64 stitches

BACK-STITCH	CROSS-STITCH	DMC #	
———		310	Black
	S	317	Pewter Gray
	N	318	Light Steel Gray
	●	413	Dark Pewter Gray
	X	414	Dark Steel Gray
	I	415	Pearl Gray
	/	762	Very Light Pearl Gray
	·		White

PAGODA SHELL ▶

42 stitches by 98 stitches

BACK-STITCH	CROSS-STITCH	DMC #	
———		310	Black
	X	317	Pewter Gray
	S	318	Light Steel Gray
	●	413	Dark Pewter Gray
	V	414	Dark Steel Gray
	—	415	Pearl Gray
	I	762	Very Light Pearl Gray
	▲	926	Dark Blue Gray
	N	927	Medium Gray Blue
	/	928	Light Gray Blue
	·		White

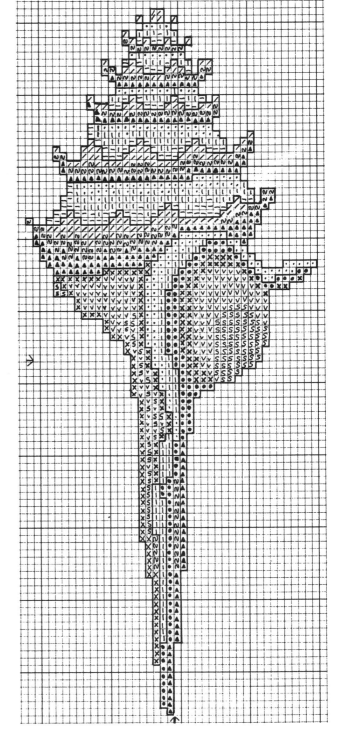

◀ JAPAN LATIAXIS

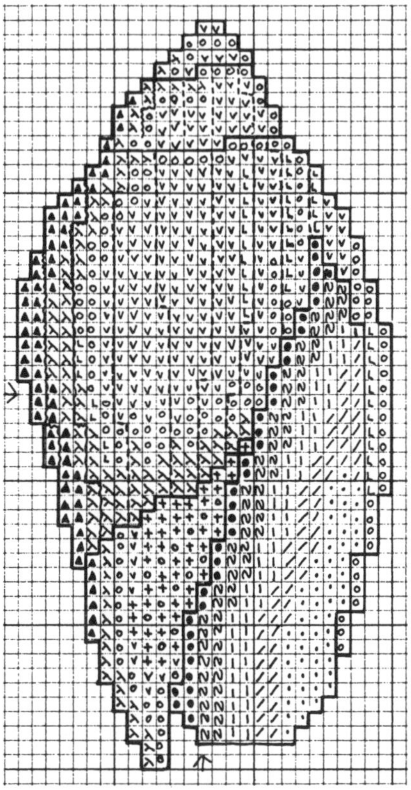

▲ ELLIOT'S VOLUTE

27 stitches by 52 stitches

BACK-STITCH	CROSS-STITCH	DMC #	
〰		300	Very Dark Mahogany
- - - -		301	Medium Mahogany
—		310	Black
	▲	640	Very Dark Beige Gray
	λ	642	Dark Beige Gray
	o	644	Medium Beige Gray
	+	746	Off White
	V	822	Light Beige Gray
	●	839	Dark Beige Brown
	N	840	Medium Beige Brown
	I	841	Light Beige Brown
	/	842	Very Light Beige Brown
	L	951	Very Light Apricot
	·		Ecru

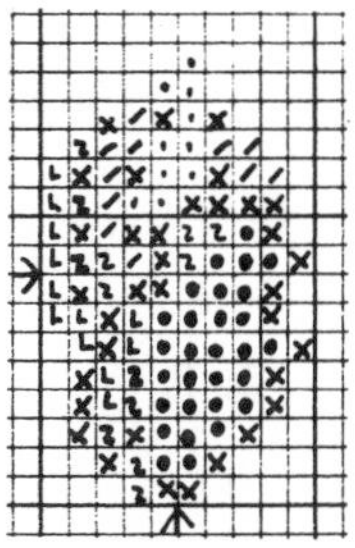

BLACKBERRY DRUPE ▶

10 stitches by 16 stitches

CROSS-STITCH	DMC #	
●	310	Black
L	420	Dark Hazelnut Brown
Z	543	Ultra Very Light Beige Brown
X	801	Dark Coffee Brown
/	3046	Medium Yellow Beige
·	3047	Light Yellow Beige

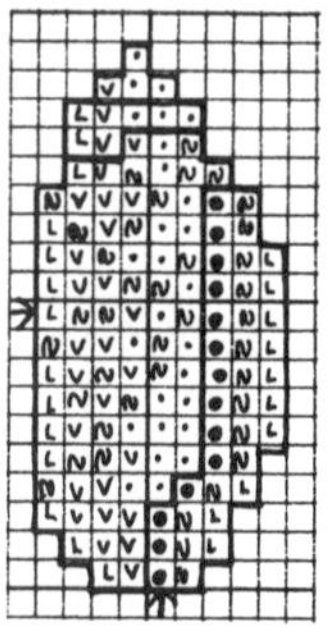

NETTED OLIVE ▶

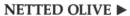

9 stitches by 19 stitches

BACK-STITCH	CROSS-STITCH	DMC #	
	·	225	Very Light Shell Pink
—		310	Black
	N	315	Dark Antique Mauve
	L	316	Medium Antique Mauve
	V	778	Light Antique Mauve
	●	3371	Black Brown

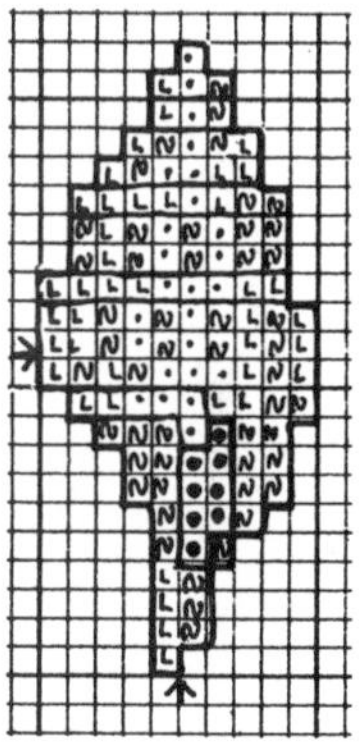

PELICAN'S FOOT ▶

10 stitches by 22 stitches

BACK-STITCH	CROSS-STITCH	DMC #	
—	●	310	Black
	L	434	Light Brown
	·	437	Light Tan
	N	801	Dark Coffee Brown

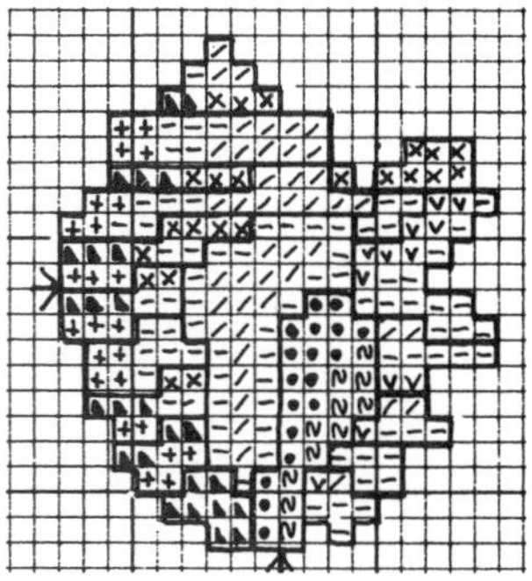

FINGER DRUPE ▶

18 stitches by 20 stitches

BACK-STITCH	CROSS-STITCH	DMC #	
—		310	Black
	V	402	Very Light Mahogany
	N	434	Light Brown
	◣	642	Dark Beige Gray
	X	644	Medium Beige Gray
	·	822	Light Beige Gray
	—	945	Light Apricot
	+	950	Light Cocoa Brown
	/	951	Very Light Apricot
	●	3371	Black Brown

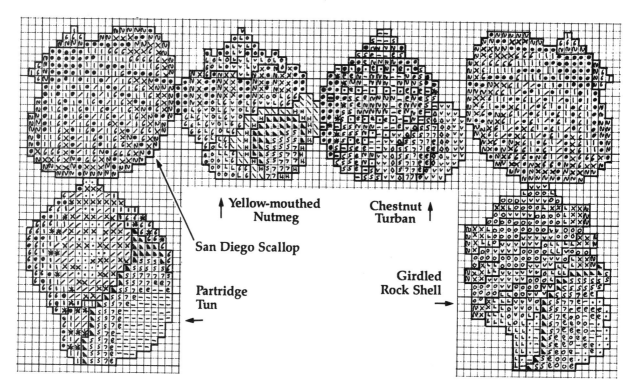

↑ Yellow-mouthed Nutmeg

Chestnut Turban ↑

San Diego Scallop

Partridge Tun ←

Girdled Rock Shell →

▲ MIXED BORDER

84 stitches by 47 stitches

BACK-STITCH	CROSS-STITCH	DMC #	
—		310	Black
	7	318	Light Steel Gray
	L	402	Very Light Mahogany
	◣	413	Dark Pewter Gray
	S	414	Dark Steel Gray
	e	415	Pearl Gray
	N	433	Medium Brown
	X	435	Very Light Brown
	6	437	Light Tan
	H	720	Dark Bittersweet

BACK-STITCH	CROSS-STITCH	DMC #	
	◹	721	Bittersweet
	◻	738	Very Light Tan
	╱	739	Fawn Beige
	─	762	Very Light Pearl Gray
	✳	801	Dark Coffee Brown
	●	898	Very Dark Coffee Brown
	o	945	Light Apricot
	◊	950	Light Cocoa Brown
	V	951	Very Light Apricot
	·		White

HAWK-WING CONCH ▶

28 stitches by 48 stitches

BACK-STITCH	CROSS-STITCH	DMC #	
—		310	Black
	◻	402	Very Light Mahogany
	●	433	Medium Brown
	S	434	Light Brown
	X	435	Very Light Brown
	L	436	Tan
	◻	543	Ultra Very Light Beige Brown
	·	712	Cream
	╱	738	Very Light Tan
	◣	839	Dark Beige Brown
	N	840	Medium Beige Brown
	⋈	841	Light Beige Brown
	─	842	Very Light Beige Brown
	V	945	Light Apricot
	+	951	Very Light Apricot

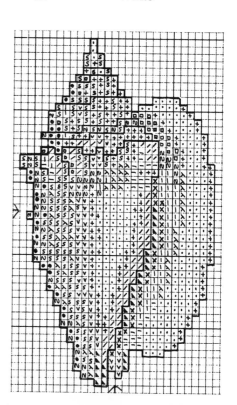

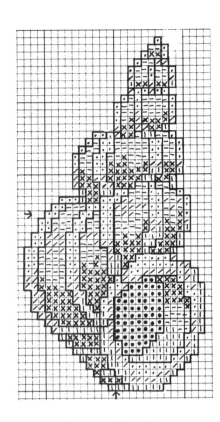

▲ PRECIOUS WENTLETRAP

26 stitches by 49 stitches

BACK-STITCH	CROSS-STITCH	DMC #	
	I	676	Light Old Gold
	/	677	Very Light Old Gold
	X	680	Dark Old Gold
	–	729	Medium Old Gold
	•	746	Off White
——		3031	Very Dark Mocha Brown
	●	3371	Black Brown

CALICO CLAM ▶

47 stitches by 49 stitches

BACK-STITCH	CROSS-STITCH	DMC #	
	●	433	Medium Brown
——	N	434	Light Brown
	X	436	Tan
	–	437	Light Tan
	•	712	Cream
	I	738	Very Light Tan
	/	739	Fawn Beige

▼ ATLANTIC PARTRIDGE TUN

21 stitches by 30 stitches

BACK-STITCH	CROSS-STITCH	DMC #	
——		310	Black
	3	402	Very Light Mahogany
	N	433	Medium Brown
	X	434	Light Brown
	I	436	Tan
	/	437	Light Tan
	•	712	Cream
	●	801	Dark Coffee Brown
	V	945	Light Apricot
	–	951	Very Light Apricot

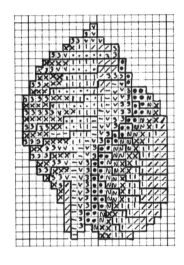

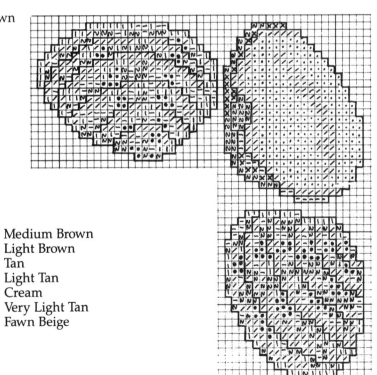

CONVEX SLIPPER ▶

30 stitches by 7 stitches

BACK-STITCH	CROSS-STITCH	DMC #	
——		310	Black
	◿	746	Off White
	⊟	3023	Light Brown Gray
	◉	3045	Dark Yellow Beige
	Ͷ	3046	Medium Yellow Beige
	☒	3047	Light Yellow Beige

▲ GENERAL CONE

27 stitches by 52 stitches

BACK-STITCH	CROSS-STITCH	DMC #	
——		310	Black
	S	317	Pewter Gray
	h	318	Light Steel Gray
	⊟	415	Pearl Gray
	◿	762	Very Light Pearl Gray
	☒	838	Very Dark Beige Brown
	Ͷ	839	Dark Beige Brown
	○	840	Medium Beige Brown
	●	898	Very Dark Coffee Brown
	Ⅱ	945	Light Apricot
	▲	975	Dark Golden Brown
	Z	976	Medium Golden Brown
	L	977	Light Golden Brown
	·		White

▼ TAPESTRY TURBAN

39 stitches by 41 stitches

BACK-STITCH	CROSS-STITCH	DMC #	
——		310	Black
	▲	839	Dark Beige Brown
	Ͷ	840	Medium Beige Brown
	○	841	Light Beige Brown
	⊟	842	Very Light Beige Brown
	✳	926*	Dark Gray Blue
	S	927*	Medium Gray Blue
	·	928*	Light Gray Blue
	◣	975	Dark Golden Brown
	L	976	Medium Golden Brown
	◿	977	Light Golden Brown
	●	991	Dark Aquamarine
	☒	992	Aquamarine
	Ⅱ	993	Light Aquamarine
	V		White

*For an iridescent effect, combine 1 strand of Balger #032 Pearl Blending Filament with each of these colors.

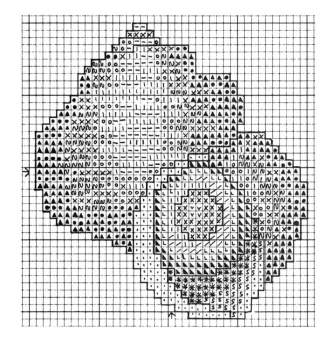

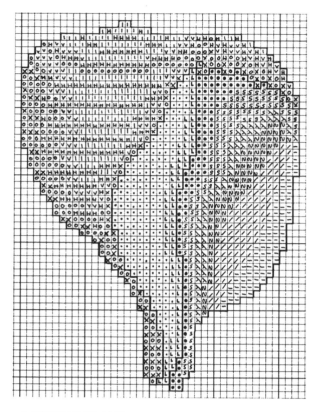

▲ PAPERY RAPA

43 stitches by 55 stitches

BACK-STITCH	CROSS-STITCH	DMC #	
——		310	Black
	λ	610	Very Dark Drab Brown
	∼	611	Dark Drab Brown
	∕	612	Medium Drab Brown
	V	676	Light Old Gold
	∣	677	Very Light Old Gold
	o	729	Medium Old Gold
	L	762	Very Light Pearl Gray
	●	938	Ultra Dark Coffee Brown
	H	3022	Medium Brown Gray
	X	3023	Light Brown Gray
	S	3031	Very Dark Mocha Brown
	⊟	3033	Very Light Mocha Brown
	·		White

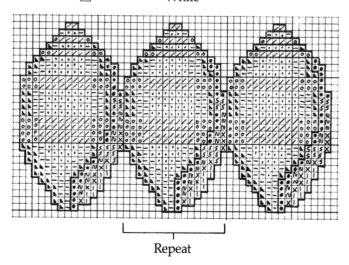

Repeat

▼ MAGELLANIC TROPHON

45 stitches by 52 stitches

BACK-STITCH	CROSS-STITCH	DMC #	
——		310	Black
	H	434	Light Brown
	V	435	Very Light Brown
	⊟	437	Light Tan
	X	646	Dark Beaver Gray
	Ʒ	647	Medium Beaver Gray
	7	648	Light Beaver Gray
	·	712	Cream
	∣	738	Very Light Tan
	∕	739	Fawn Beige
	L	762	Very Light Pearl Gray
	◣	801	Dark Coffee Brown
	●	844	Ultra Dark Beaver Gray
	○	3072	Very Light Beaver Gray

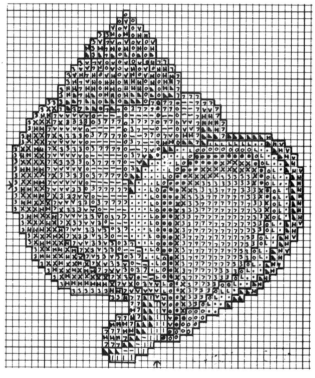

◄ COFFEE MELAMPUS

16 stitch repeat by 28 stitches

BACK-STITCH	CROSS-STITCH	DMC #	
——		310	Black
	∼	433	Medium Brown
	X	434	Light Brown
	∣	436	Tan
	S	720	Dark Bittersweet
	o	721	Bittersweet
	∕	722	Medium Bittersweet
	·	725	Topaz
	◣	782	Medium Topaz
	⊟	783	Christmas Gold
	●	898	Very Dark Coffee Brown

29

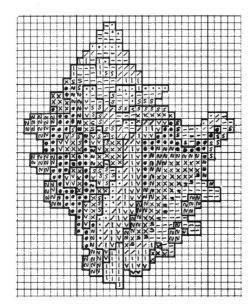

▲ PACIFIC HORSE CHESTNUT

32 stitches by 39 stitches

BACK-STITCH	CROSS-STITCH	DMC #	
——		310	Black
	V	407	Medium Cocoa Brown
	●	838	Very Dark Beige Brown
	N	839	Dark Beige Brown
	X	840	Medium Beige Brown
	S	841	Light Beige Brown
	—	842	Very Light Beige Brown
	/	945	Light Apricot
	I	950	Light Cocoa Brown
	·	951	Very Light Apricot

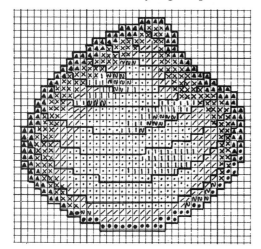

▲ HARD SHELL CLAM

34 stitches by 31 stitches

BACK-STITCH	CROSS-STITCH	DMC #	
——		310	Black
	/	676	Light Old Gold
	·	677	Very Light Old Gold
	N	680	Dark Old Gold
	I	729	Medium Old Gold
	▲	730	Very Dark Olive Green
	X	732	Olive Green
	●	869	Very Dark Hazelnut Brown

▼ CHANNELED TURBAN

26 stitches by 31 stitches

BACK-STITCH	CROSS-STITCH	DMC #	
——		310	Black
	6	318	Light Steel Gray
	Z	402	Very Light Mahogany
	X	415	Pearl Gray
	S	640*	Very Dark Beige Gray
	M	642*	Dark Beige Gray
	3	644*	Medium Beige Gray
	/	677	Very Light Old Gold
	·	712	Cream
	—	739	Fawn Beige
	I	822*	Light Beige Gray
	●	839	Dark Beige Brown
	N	840	Medium Beige Brown
	+	841	Light Beige Brown
	V	945	Light Apricot

*For an iridescent effect, combine 1 strand of Balger #032 Pearl Blending Filament with each of these colors.

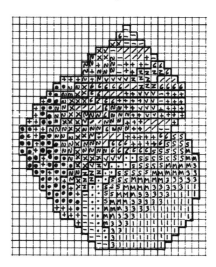

GIANT SPIDER CONCH ▶

84 stitches by 120 stitches

CROSS-STITCH	DMC #	
▲	223	Dark Shell Pink
◣	300	Very Dark Mahogany
Z	301	Medium Dark Mahogany
N	317	Pewter Gray
/	318	Light Steel Gray
X	335	Rose
●	413	Dark Pewter Gray
+	414	Dark Steel Gray
L	415	Pearl Gray
O	762	Very Light Pearl Gray
—	776	Medium Pink
V	818	Baby Pink
I	819	Light Baby Pink
3	899	Medium Rose
S	3326	Light Rose
7	3688	Medium Mauve
·		White

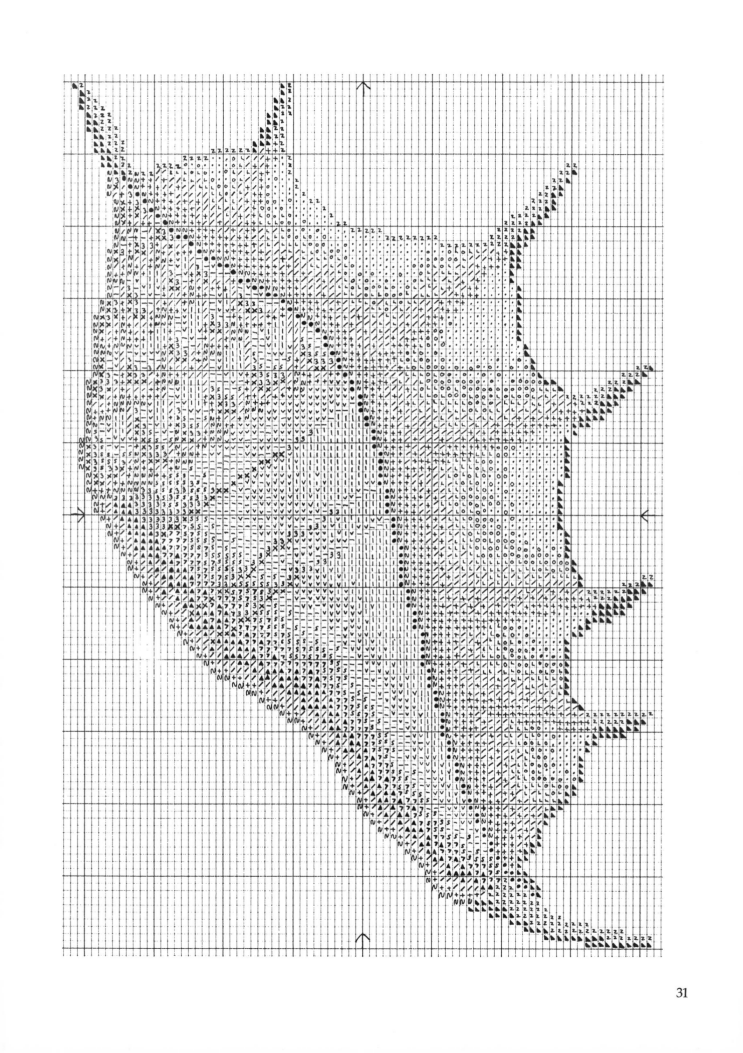

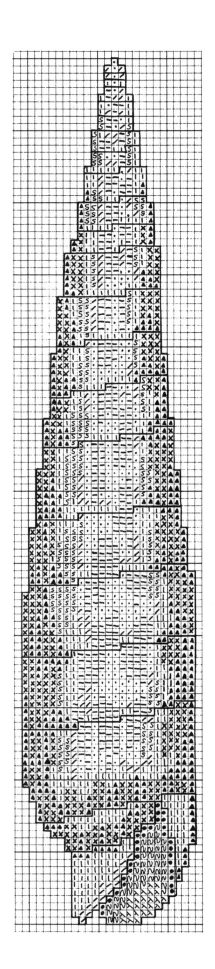

◀ FLAME AUGER

25 stitches by 120 stitches

BACK-STITCH	CROSS-STITCH	DMC #	
	❘	407	Medium Cocoa Brown
	▲	632	Chocolate
	⬤	839	Dark Beige Brown
	⋂	840	Medium Beige Brown
	λ	841	Light Beige Brown
—		898	Very Dark Coffee Brown
	╱	950	Light Cocoa Brown
	•	951	Very Light Apricot
	X	975	Dark Golden Brown
	S	976	Medium Golden Brown
	▬	977	Light Golden Brown

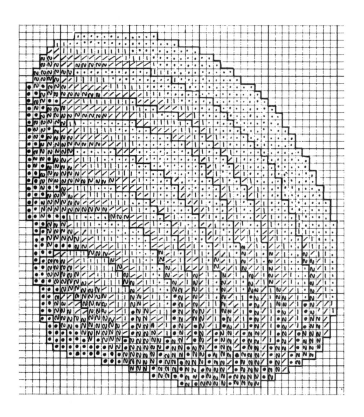

▲ SURF CLAM

45 stitches by 49 stitches

BACK-STITCH	CROSS-STITCH	DMC #	
—		310	Black
	⬤	924	Very Dark Gray Blue
	⋂	926	Dark Gray Blue
	╱	927	Medium Gray Blue
	❘	928	Light Gray Blue
	•		White

CARDINAL MITER ▶

34 stitches by 47 stitches

	DMC #	
⊞	433	Medium Brown
☑	434	Light Brown
☐	435	Very Light Brown
÷	436	Tan
❘	437	Light Tan
⑤	720	Dark Bittersweet
╱	721	Bittersweet
⊙	722	Medium Bittersweet
·	738	Very Light Tan
⚆	801	Dark Coffee Brown
☒	840	Medium Beige Brown
✳	841	Light Beige Brown
▲	920	Medium Copper
⊙	938	Ultra Dark Coffee Brown

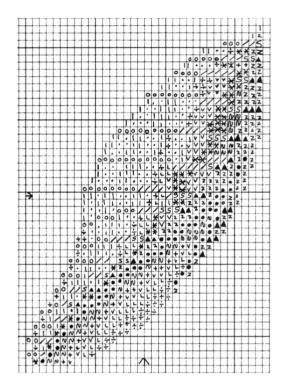

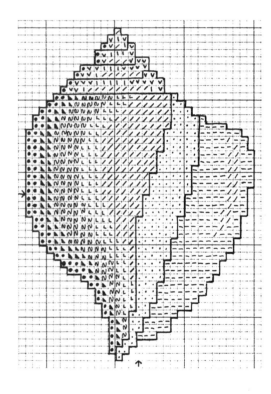

BEAUTIFUL TELLIN ▶

20-stitch by 16-stitch repeat

BACK-STITCH	CROSS-STITCH	DMC #	
	⚄	720	Dark Bittersweet
	╱	721	Bittersweet
	·	722	Medium Bittersweet
——		918	Dark Red Copper
	⊙	920	Medium Copper

For an iridescent effect, combine 1 strand of Balger #100 White Blending Filament with all colors.

◀ DOG CONCH

33 stitches by 46 stitches

BACK-STITCH	CROSS-STITCH	DMC #	
	·	676*	Light Old Gold
	⊟	712	Cream
	⊙	869	Very Dark Hazelnut Brown
——		898	Very Dark Coffee Brown
	☑	976	Medium Golden Brown
	❘	977	Light Golden Brown
	◣	3045	Dark Yellow Beige
	⚄	3046	Medium Yellow Beige
	☐	3047	Light Yellow Beige
	╱		Ecru

*For an iridescent effect, combine 1 strand of Balger #013 Beige Blending Filament with this color.

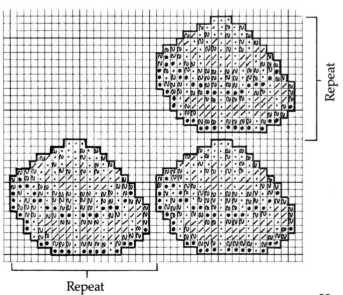

LUNATE CRASSINELLA ▶

17 stitches by 15 stitches

DMC #

⊡	822	Light Beige Gray
⦿	838	Very Dark Beige Brown
N	839	Dark Beige Brown
X	840	Medium Beige Brown
I	841	Light Beige Brown
⁄	842	Very Light Beige Brown

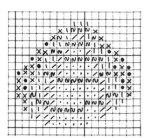

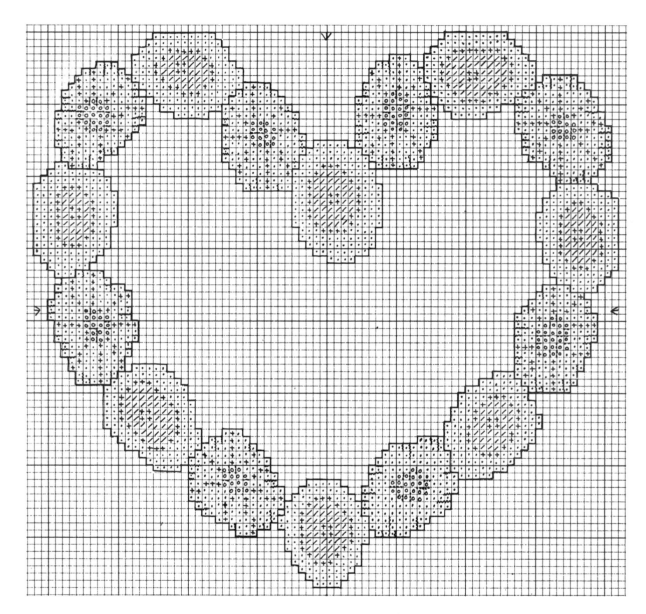

▲ EIGHT-RIBBED LIMPET

84 stitches by 77 stitches

BACK-STITCH	CROSS-STITCH	DMC #		BACK-STITCH	CROSS-STITCH	DMC #	
——		310	Black		⊡	712	Cream
	⊞	415	Pearl Gray		⁄	739	Fawn Beige
----		433	Medium Brown	∿∿		938	Ultra Dark Coffee Brown
	⊙	437	Light Tan				

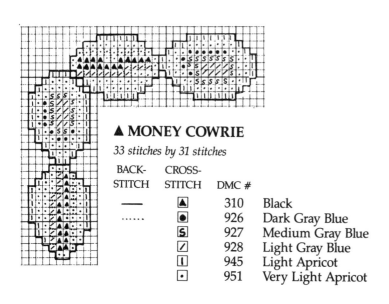

▲ MONEY COWRIE

33 stitches by 31 stitches

BACK-STITCH	CROSS-STITCH	DMC #	
——	▲	310	Black
......	●	926	Dark Gray Blue
	S	927	Medium Gray Blue
	/	928	Light Gray Blue
	I	945	Light Apricot
	·	951	Very Light Apricot

▼ PRICKLY COCKLE

51 stitches by 50 stitches

BACK-STITCH	CROSS-STITCH	DMC #	
——		310	Black
	/	647	Medium Beaver Gray
	S	648	Light Beaver Gray
	·	712	Cream
	I	3607	Dark Fuchsia
	Z	3608	Fuchsia
	N	3609	Light Fuchsia
	●	3685	Dark Mauve
	X	3687	Mauve
	O	3688	Medium Mauve
	—	3689	Light Mauve

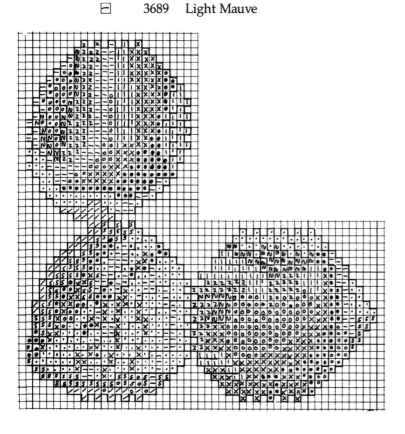

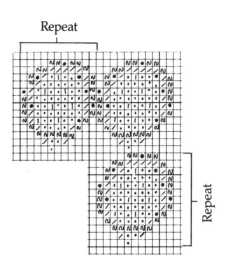

DWARF PERIWINKLE ▲

11-stitch by 13-stitch repeat

CROSS-STITCH	DMC #	
N	611	Dark Drab Brown
I	612	Medium Drab Brown
●	926	Dark Gray Blue
/	927	Medium Gray Blue
·	928	Light Gray Blue

VIRGIN NERITE ▼

20-stitch by 27-stitch repeat

BACK-STITCH	CROSS-STITCH	DMC #	
	I	451	Dark Shell Gray
	—	453	Light Shell Gray
	·	712	Cream
	/	762	Very Light Pearl Gray
∿∿	●	924	Very Dark Gray Blue
	N	926	Dark Gray Blue
	L	927	Medium Gray Blue
	O	928	Light Gray Blue
	V	945	Light Apricot
	S	948	Very Light Peach

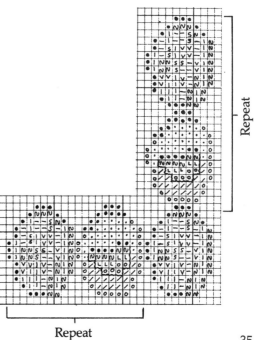

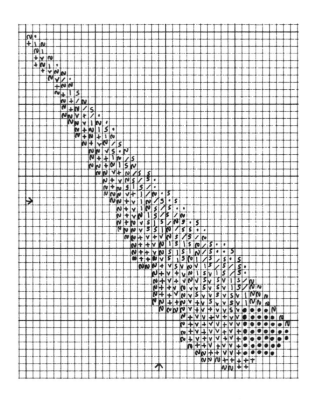

AUGER SCREW SHELL ◀

38 stitches by 47 stitches

DMC #

S	434	Light Brown
V	436	Tan
I	437	Light Tan
∕	738	Very Light Tan
•	739	Fawn Beige
⊞	801	Dark Coffee Brown
N	898	Very Dark Coffee Brown
⦿	3371	Black Brown

MARLINSPIKE ▶

35 stitches by 48 stitches

DMC #

Z	301	Medium Dark Mahogany
▲	400	Dark Mahogany
S	402	Very Light Mahogany
⊞	922	Light Copper
I	945	Light Apricot
∕	951	Very Light Apricot
N	975	Dark Golden Brown
V	976	Medium Golden Brown
−	977	Light Golden Brown
⦿	3371	Black Brown

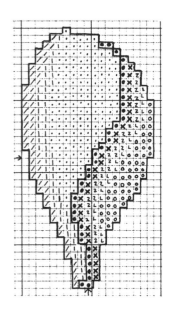

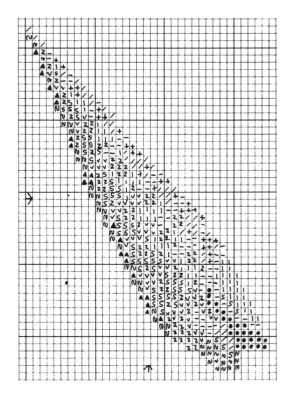

ATLANTIC FIG SHELL ◀

19 stitches by 36 stitches

BACK-STITCH	CROSS-STITCH	DMC #	
	☒	317	Pewter Gray
	Z	318	Light Steel Gray
—	⦿	413	Dark Pewter Gray
	L	415	Pearl Gray
	∕	437	Light Tan
	•	712	Cream
	I	739	Fawn Beige
	◙	762	Very Light Pearl Gray

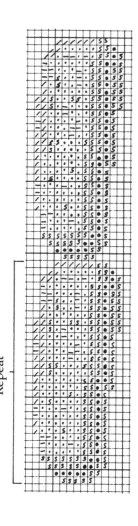

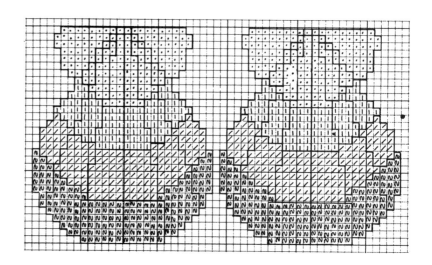

▲ SWIFT'S SCALLOP

53 stitches by 30 stitches

BACK-STITCH	CROSS-STITCH	DMC #	
—		310	Black
	Ⓝ	335	Rose
	·	776	Medium Pink
	/	899	Medium Rose
	Ⅰ	3326	Light Rose

◀ ROSE-SPOTTED SOLEN

13-stitch by 31-stitch repeat

	DMC #	
S	221	Dark Shell Pink
−	223	Medium Dark Shell Pink
/	224	Medium Shell Pink
·	225	Light Shell Pink
⦿	300	Very Dark Mahogany

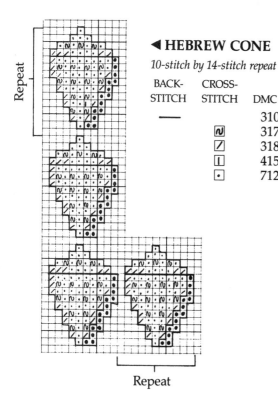

◀ HEBREW CONE

10-stitch by 14-stitch repeat

BACK-STITCH	CROSS-STITCH	DMC #	
—		310	Black
	Ⓝ	317	Pewter Gray
	/	318	Light Steel Gray
	Ⅰ	415	Pearl Gray
	·	712	Cream

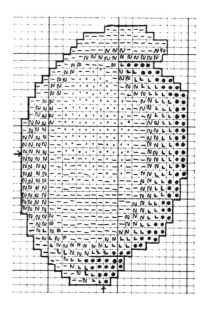

EGG COWRIE ▲

24 stitches by 36 stitches

BACK-STITCH	CROSS-STITCH	DMC #	
—		310	Black
	⦿	318	Light Steel Gray
	Ⓝ	414	Dark Steel Gray
	Ⅼ	415	Pearl Gray
	−	762	Very Light Pearl Gray
	·		White

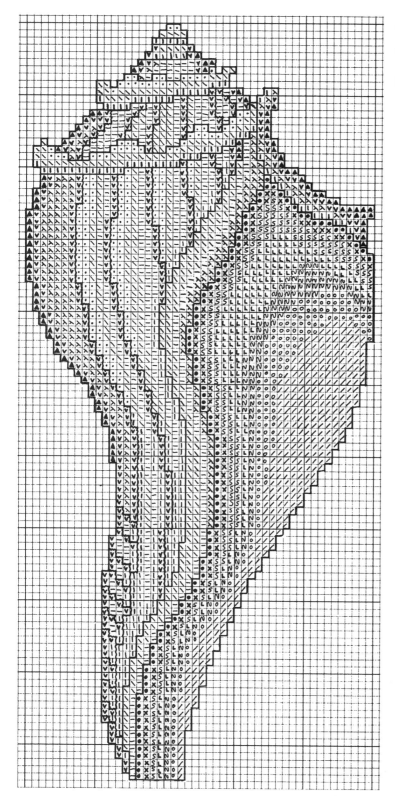

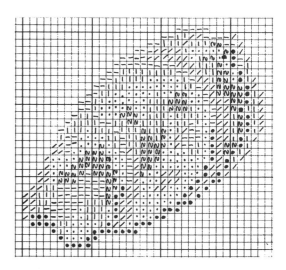

◄ KNOBBED WHELK

50 stitches by 105 stitches

BACK-STITCH	CROSS-STITCH	DMC #	
——		310	Black
	⊠	402	Very Light Mahogany
~~	▲	451	Dark Shell Gray
	∨	452	Medium Shell Gray
	Ι	453	Light Shell Gray
	·	712	Cream
	⧄	721	Bittersweet
	◉	722	Medium Bittersweet
	●	918	Dark Red Copper
	✕	919	Red Copper
	S	920	Medium Copper
	L	921	Copper
	N	922	Light Copper
	−	945	Light Apricot
	◣	951	Very Light Apricot

▲ EASTERN OYSTER

35 stitches by 31 stitches

	DMC #	
Ι	402	Very Light Mahogany
−	646	Dark Beaver Gray
⧄	648	Light Beaver Gray
Ͷ	676	Light Old Gold
·	712	Cream
●	844	Ultra Dark Beaver Gray

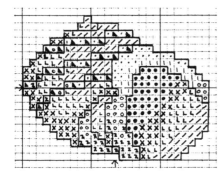

BUTTERFLY MOON

27 stitches by 20 stitches

BACK-STITCH	CROSS-STITCH	DMC #	
——	◣	310	Black
	Z	317	Pewter Gray
	O	318	Light Steel Gray
	▯	415	Pearl Gray
	●	838	Very Dark Beige Brown
	X	839	Dark Beige Brown
	L	840	Medium Beige Brown
	╱	841	Light Beige Brown
	·		White

SOUTHERN MOON SNAIL ▶

37 stitches by 26 stitches

BACK-STITCH	CROSS-STITCH	DMC #	
——		310	Black
	N	420	Dark Hazelnut Brown
	O	676	Light Old Gold
	·	677	Very Light Old Gold
	X	680	Dark Old Gold
	L	729	Medium Old Gold
	●	869	Very Dark Hazelnut Brown

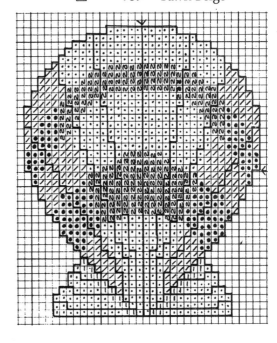

◀ COMMON PAPER NAUTILUS

45 stitches by 35 stitches

BACK-STITCH	CROSS-STITCH	DMC #	
——	●	434	Light Brown
	X	435	Very Light Brown
	S	437	Light Tan
	·	712	Cream
	╱	738	Very Light Tan
	▯	739	Fawn Beige

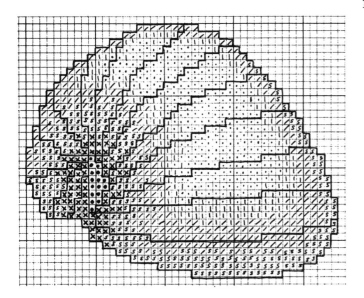

NOBLE SCALLOP ▶

34 stitches by 40 stitches

BACK-STITCH	CROSS-STITCH	DMC #	
	●	208	Very Dark Lavender
	S	209	Dark Lavender
	▯	210	Medium Lavender
	·	211	Light Lavender
——		550	Very Dark Violet

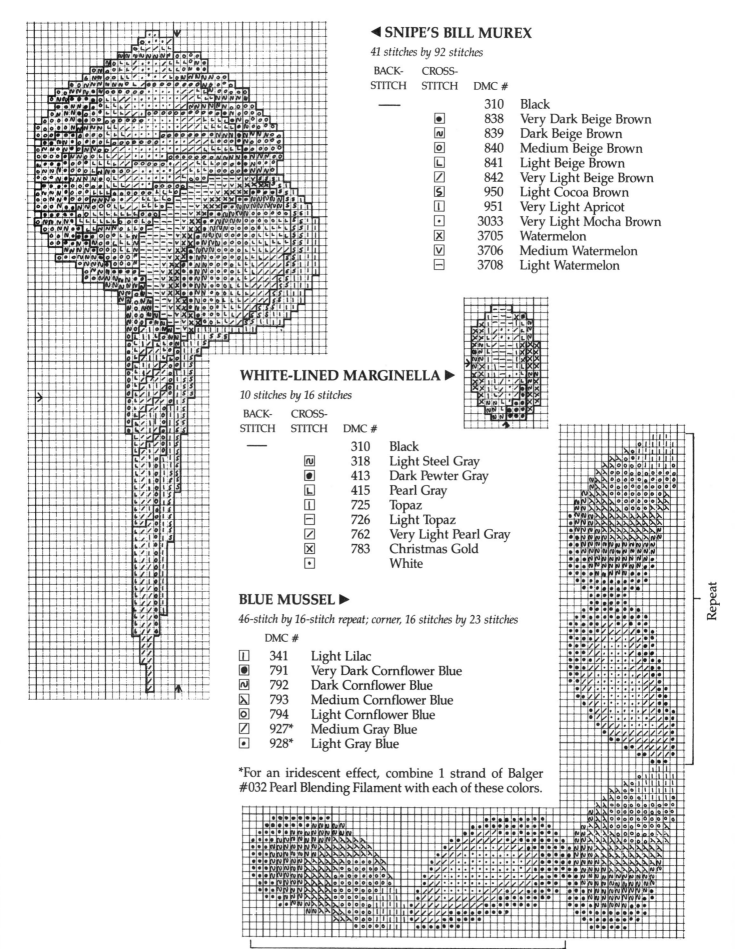

◄ SNIPE'S BILL MUREX

41 stitches by 92 stitches

BACK-STITCH	CROSS-STITCH	DMC #	
——		310	Black
	●	838	Very Dark Beige Brown
	Ν	839	Dark Beige Brown
	ο	840	Medium Beige Brown
	L	841	Light Beige Brown
	∕	842	Very Light Beige Brown
	S	950	Light Cocoa Brown
	I	951	Very Light Apricot
	·	3033	Very Light Mocha Brown
	X	3705	Watermelon
	V	3706	Medium Watermelon
	−	3708	Light Watermelon

WHITE-LINED MARGINELLA ►

10 stitches by 16 stitches

BACK-STITCH	CROSS-STITCH	DMC #	
——		310	Black
	Ν	318	Light Steel Gray
	●	413	Dark Pewter Gray
	L	415	Pearl Gray
	I	725	Topaz
	−	726	Light Topaz
	∕	762	Very Light Pearl Gray
	X	783	Christmas Gold
	·		White

BLUE MUSSEL ►

46-stitch by 16-stitch repeat; corner, 16 stitches by 23 stitches

	DMC #	
I	341	Light Lilac
●	791	Very Dark Cornflower Blue
Ν	792	Dark Cornflower Blue
⋋	793	Medium Cornflower Blue
ο	794	Light Cornflower Blue
∕	927*	Medium Gray Blue
·	928*	Light Gray Blue

*For an iridescent effect, combine 1 strand of Balger #032 Pearl Blending Filament with each of these colors.

Repeat

Repeat

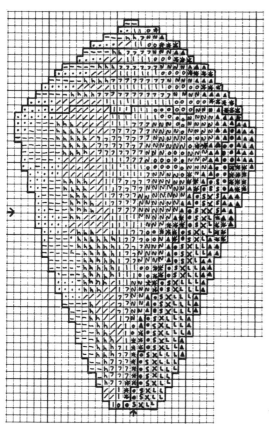

◀ STRIATE CONE

35 stitches by 54 stitches

BACK-STITCH	CROSS-STITCH	DMC #	
———		310	Black
	S	317	Pewter Gray
	L	318	Light Steel Gray
	●	413	Dark Pewter Gray
	X	414	Dark Steel Gray
	N	433	Medium Brown
	7	434	Light Brown
	h	436	Tan
	—	437	Light Tan
	I	725	Topaz
	/	726	Light Topaz
	·	727	Very Light Topaz
	✳	782	Medium Topaz
	O	783	Christmas Gold
	▲	801	Dark Coffee Brown

▼ ATLANTIC COQUINA

74 stitches by 56 stitches

CROSS-STITCH	DMC #	
/	434	Light Brown
I	436	Tan
V	597	Turquoise
e	598	Light Turquoise
■	720	Dark Bittersweet
O	721	Bittersweet
+	722	Medium Bittersweet
N	725	Topaz
—	738	Very Light Tan
·	739	Fawn Beige
●	782	Medium Topaz
L	783	Christmas Gold
✳	806	Dark Peacock Blue
◣	926	Dark Gray Blue
S	927	Medium Gray Blue
⋈	928	Light Gray Blue
▲	975	Dark Golden Brown
Z	976	Medium Golden Brown
J	977	Light Golden Brown

SEAWEED

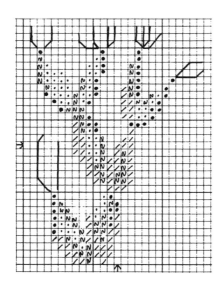

▲ 25 stitches by 33 stitches

BACK-STITCH	CROSS-STITCH	DMC #	
———	●	720	Dark Bittersweet
	Ⴎ	721	Bittersweet
	·	722	Medium Bittersweet
	∕	966	Medium Baby Green

▼ 31 stitches by 37 stitches

BACK-STITCH	CROSS-STITCH	DMC #	
———		310	Black
	·	964	Light Aqua
	●	991	Dark Aquamarine
	✗	992	Aquamarine
	⊡	993	Light Aquamarine

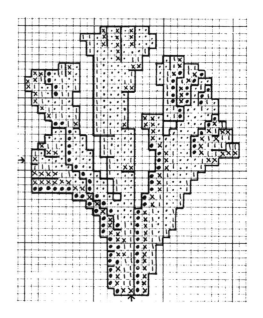

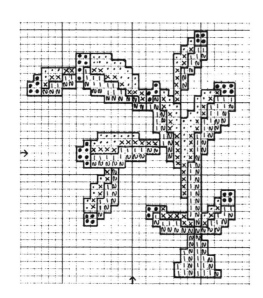

▲ 30 stitches by 34 stitches

BACK-STITCH	CROSS-STITCH	DMC #	
———		310	Black
	●	327	Dark Antique Violet
	⊡	407	Medium Cocoa Brown
	Ⴎ	632	Chocolate
	✗	3041	Medium Antique Violet
	·	3042	Light Antique Violet

▼ 21 stitches by 34 stitches

	DMC #	
⊡	471	Light Avocado Green
✗	472	Very Light Avocado Green

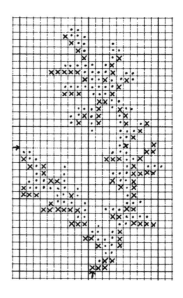

CORALS

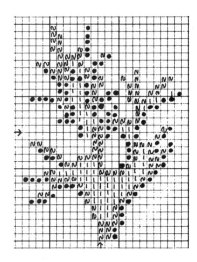

▲ *23 stitches by 30 stitches*

	DMC #	
◉	975	Dark Golden Brown
Ⓝ	976	Medium Golden Brown
Ⓘ	977	Light Golden Brown

▼ *23 stitches by 36 stitches*

	DMC #	
Ⓝ	760	Salmon
◪	761	Light Salmon
⊡	945	Light Apricot
◣	3328	Medium Salmon

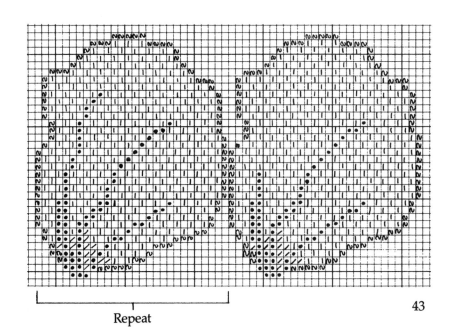

▼ *17 stitches by 33 stitches*

BACK-STITCH	CROSS-STITCH	DMC #	
—		310	Black
	Ⓝ	407	Medium Cocoa Brown
	◣	632	Chocolate
	⊡	950	Light Cocoa Brown
	Ⓢ	3347	Medium Yellow Green
	◪	3348	Light Yellow Green

▼ SEA FAN CORAL

28-stitch repeat by 34 stitches

	DMC #	
◉	208	Very Dark Lavender
Ⓝ	209	Dark Lavender
◪	210	Medium Lavender
Ⓘ	211	Light Lavender

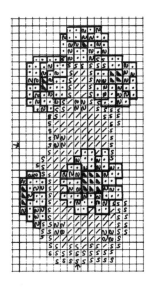

Repeat

43

SAND DOLLARS

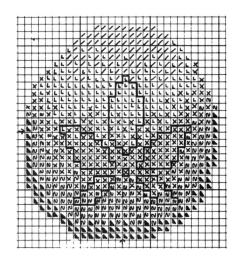

◄ *28 stitches by 30 stitches*

BACK-STITCH	CROSS-STITCH	DMC #	
——		310	Black
	L	518	Light Wedgwood Blue
	∕	519	Sky Blue
	◣	824	Very Dark Blue
	N	825	Dark Blue
	X	826	Medium Blue

31 stitches by 32 stitches ►

BACK-STITCH	CROSS-STITCH	DMC #	
——		310	Black
	Z	958	Dark Aqua
	∕	959	Aqua
	·	964	Light Aqua
	◣	991	Dark Aquamarine

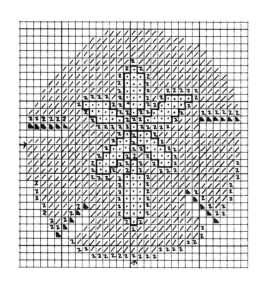

◄ *37 stitches by 35 stitches*

BACK-STITCH	CROSS-STITCH	DMC #	
——		310	Black
	●	730	Very Dark Olive Green
	N	732	Olive Green
	∕	733	Medium Olive Green
	·	734	Light Olive Green

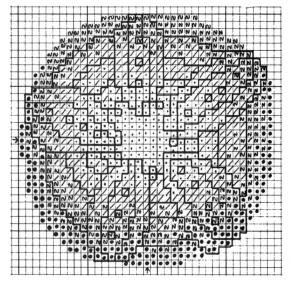

SAND DOLLARS

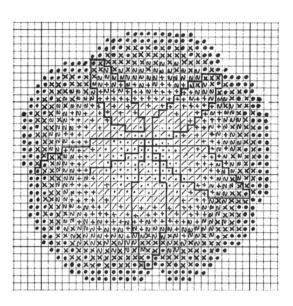

36 stitches by 35 stitches ▶

BACK-STITCH	CROSS-STITCH	DMC #	
——		310	Black
	⊙	829	Dark Greenish Brown
	☒	830	Medium Greenish Brown
	Ⓝ	831	Light Greenish Brown
	⊞	832	Dark Golden Wheat
	⧄	833	Medium Golden Wheat
	⊡	834	Light Golden Wheat

◀ *26 stitches by 32 stitches*

BACK-STITCH	CROSS-STITCH	DMC #	
——		310	Black
	⊙	315	Dark Antique Mauve
	①	316	Medium Antique Mauve
	⊞	632	Chocolate
	⊡	778	Light Antique Mauve
	⧄	3064	Spice

33 stitches by 32 stitches ▶

BACK-STITCH	CROSS-STITCH	DMC #	
——		310	Black
	⧄	725	Topaz
	⊡	726	Light Topaz
	⊙	782	Medium Topaz
	Ⓝ	783	Christmas Gold

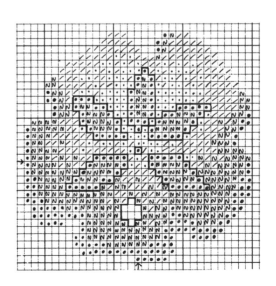

35 stitches by 33 stitches ▶

DMC #

Ⱳ	349	Dark Coral
☒	350	Medium Coral
Ⅱ	351	Coral
·	352	Light Coral
◉	817	Very Dark Coral

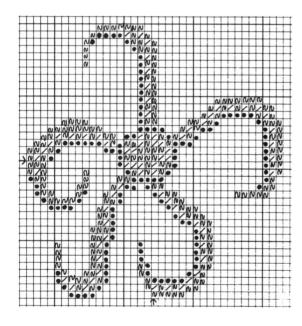

◀ *37 stitches by 38 stitches*

DMC #

◉	700	Bright Christmas Green
Ⱳ	702	Kelly Green
⧄	704	Bright Chartreuse

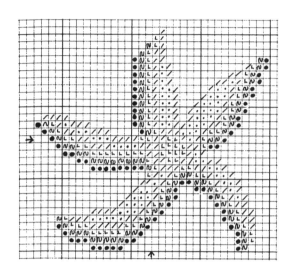

◀ *34 stitches by 31 stitches*

DMC #

◪	725	Topaz
·	726	Light Topaz
●	780	Very Dark Topaz
ℕ	782	Medium Topaz
Ⓛ	783	Christmas Gold

30 stitches by 30 stitches ▶

DMC #

Ⓛ	209	Dark Lavender
●	333	Dark Lilac
ℕ	340	Lilac
·	341	Light Lilac

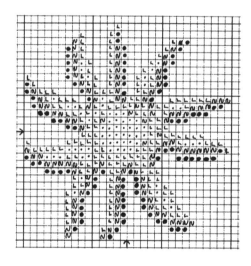

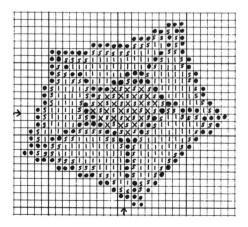

◀ *30 stitches by 26 stitches*

DMC #

●	561	Dark Sea Foam Green
⊠	562	Sea Foam Green
⑤	563	Medium Sea Foam Green
Ⅱ	564	Light Sea Foam Green

SIX STRAND EMBROIDERY COTTON (FLOSS) CONVERSION CHART

KEY: T = Possible Substitute   * = Close Match   — = No Match

DMC NO.	ROYAL MOULINÉ NO.	BATES/ANCHOR NO.
White	1001	2
Ecru	8600	926
208	3335*	110*
209	3415*	105
210	3320*	104
211	3410	108*
221	2570	897*
223	2555	894
224	2545	893
225	2540	892
300	8330	352*
301	8315*	349*
304	2415*	47*
307	6005*	289*
309	2525*	42*
310	1002	403
311	4275T	149*
312	—	147*
315	3130	896*
316	3120	895*
317	1030*	400*
318	1020*	399*
319	5025	246*
320	5015	216*
321	2415	47
322	—	978*
326	2530*	59*
327	3365*	101*
333	—	119
334	4250T	145
335	2525T	42*
336	4270*	149*
340	—	118
341	—	117
347	2425*	13*
349	2400	13
350	2045T	11*
351	2015T	11*
352	2015*	10*
353	2010*	8*
355	8095	5968
356	8090	5975*
367	5020	216*
368	5005*	240*
369	5005	213*
370	—	889*
371	—	888*
372	—	887*
400	8325*	351
402	8305*	347*
407	8005	882*
413	1025*	401
414	1020*	400*
415	1015	398
420	8720*	375*
422	8710*	373*
433	8265	371*
434	8215	309
435	8210*	369*
436	8205	363*
437	8200*	362
444	6155*	291
445	6000	288
451	—	399*
452	—	399*
453	1015T	397*
469	5255	267*
470	5255*	267
471	5245	266*
472	5240	264*
498	2425T	20*
500	5125	879*
501	5120*	878
502	5110	876
503	5105	875
504	5100	213*
517	4860*	169*
518	4860*	168*
519	4855T	167*
520	—	862*
522	—	859*
523	—	859*
524	1115T	858*
535	—	401*
543	8500	933*
550	3380*	102*
552	3370	101
553	3360	98
554	3355*	96*
561	—	212*
562	—	210*
563	—	208*
564	—	203*
580	5935	267*
581	5925	266*
597	4860*	168*
598	4855*	167*
600	2225*	59*
601	2225*	78*
602	2640*	77*
603	2720*	76*
604	2710	75*
605	2155	50*
606	7260	335
608	7255	333*
610	5825T	889*
611	5735T	898
612	8815*	832
613	5605*	956*
632	8530	936*
640	8625	903
642	8620*	392
644	8800	830
645	1115	905*
646	1115*	8581
647	1110	8581*
648	1100*	900
666	2405	46
676	6250	891
677	—	886*
680	6260*	901
699	5375	923*
700	5365*	229
701	5365*	227
702	5330	239
703	5320	238
704	5310*	256*
712	8600*	387*
718	3015*	88
720	—	326
721	—	324*
722	—	323*
725	6215	306*
726	6150*	295
727	6135	293
729	6255	890
730	—	924*
731	—	281*
732	5925T	281*
733	—	280*
734	—	279*
738	8245*	942
739	8240*	885*
740	7045	316
741	6125	304
742	6120	303
743	6210	297
744	6110*	301*
745	6105	300*
746	6100	386*
747	4850	158*
754	8075	778*
758	8080	868
760	2035	9*
761	2030	8*
762	1010*	397
772	4600*	264*
775	2110*	128*
776	3110	24*
778	—	968*
780	8215	310*
781	8215	309*
782	6230	308
783	6220*	307
791	4165*	941*
792	4155T	940
793	4155	121
794	4145	120*
796	4340	133*
797	4265*	132*
798	4325	131*
799	4250*	130*
800	4310	128
801	8405	357*
806	4870T	169*
807	4860*	168*
809	4145*	130*
813	4610*	160*
814	2340T	44*
815	2530T	43
816	2530	44*
817	2415T	19
818	2505*	48
819	2000	892*
820	4345	134
822	8605*	387*
823	4400*	150
824	4225	164*
825	4215	162*
826	4210	161*
827	4605	159*
828	4850	158*
829	5825	906
830	5825*	889*
831	5825T	889*
832	5815	907
833	5815*	874*
834	5810*	874
838	8425*	380
839	8560	380*
840	8555	379*
841	8550	378*
842	8505	376*
844	1115T	401*
869	8720*	944*
890	5025*	879*
891	2135	35*
892	2130	28
893	2125*	27
894	2115T	26
895	5430*	246*
898	8425*	360
899	2515	27*
901	7230*	333
902	—	72*
904	5295*	258*
905	5295	258*
906	5285*	256*
907	5280*	255
909	5370	229*
910	5370*	228*
911	5465*	205*
912	5465	205
913	5460*	209
915	3030	89*
917	3020*	89*
918	8330*	341*
919	8095*	341*
920	8060*	339*
921	8060T	349*
922	8315T	324*
924	4830T	851*
926	4820*	779*
927	4810T	849*
928	1010T	900*
930	4510	922*
931	4505	921*
932	4500	920*
934	5070T	862*
935	5225T	862*
936	5260T	269
937	5260	268
938	8430	381
939	4405	127
943	4935*	188*
945	8020*	347*
946	7230*	332*
947	7255*	330*
948	8070	778*
950	8020T	4146
951	8020T	366*
954	5455*	203*
955	5450	206*
956	2170*	40*
957	2160T	40*
958	—	187
959	2515*	186
961	2515	76*
962	2515	76*
963	2505	49*
964	5150*	185
966	5150*	214*
970	7040	316*
971	7045	316*
972	6120*	298
973	6015	290
975	8365	355*
976	8355	308*
977	8350	307*
986	5430	246*
987	5020T	244*
988	5295T	243*
989	5405T	242*
991	5165T	189*
992	4925*	187*
993	4915*	186*
995	4710	410
996	4700	433
3011	5525T	845*
3012	5525*	844*
3013	5515	842*
3021	5430	382*
3022	—	8581*
3023	—	8581*
3024	1100	900*
3031	—	905*
3032	8620T	903*
3033	8610*	388*
3041	3215*	871
3042	3205*	869
3045	6260T	373*
3046	5810	887*
3047	5805	886*
3051	5530T	846*
3052	5060*	859*
3053	5055*	859*
3064	8005*	914*
3072	4805*	397*
3078	6130	292*
3325	4200	159*
3326	2115*	25*
3328	2045	11*
3340	—	329
3341	—	328
3345	5025T	268*
3346	5220T	257*
3347	5210*	266*
3348	5270*	265
3350	2220	42*
3354	2210	74*
3362	—	862*
3363	—	861*
3364	—	843*
3371	8435	382
3607	—	87*
3608	—	86
3609	—	85
3685	2335	70*
3687	2325	69*
3688	2320	66*
3689	2310	49
3705	—	35*
3706	—	28*
3708	—	26*
48	9000*	1201*
51	9014	1220
52	9006	1208
53	—	
57	9002	1203
61	9013T	1218*
62	9000T	1201*
67	—	1211*
69	9005*	1218*
75	9009*	1206*
90	—	1217*
91	9002	1211
92	9011T	1216*
93	9007*	1210*
94	9011*	1216
95	9006T	1208*
99	9005*	1207*
101	9009*	1213*
102	—	1208*
103	—	1210*
104	9012	1217
105	9013*	1218
106	9002T	1203*
107	9003	1204
108	9014*	1220*
111	9007*	1218*
112	9003T	1204*
113	9007*	1210*
114	9010	1215
115	9004	1206
121	9007	1210
122	9010T	1213*
123	—	1213*
124	9007T	1210*
125	9009	1213
126	9006*	1208*